Cosmic blessings as you journey into Love

The Cosmic Pilgrim

The Cosmic Pilgrim

*A Spiritual Exploration of the New Story
of Science and Religion*

※   ※   ※

MARGARET MACINTYRE

WIPF & STOCK · Eugene, Oregon

THE COSMIC PILGRIM
A Spiritual Exploration of the New Story of Science and Religion

Wipf & Stock
An Imprint of Wipf and Stock Publishers
199 W. 8th Ave., Suite 3
Eugene, OR 97401

www.wipfandstock.com

ISBN 13: 978-1-60899-271-3

Manufactured in the U.S.A.

To my sons Paul and Robbie and my husband, Dale.

Contents

Preface

I WOULD LIKE TO declare my manifesto right from the start so that the reader may have a sense of the spirituality that I am attempting to develop in this book. I believe that the Universe took form as an embryo in the womb of God, and that it is on a journey in time and space, evolving toward its fulfillment, its birth. The purpose of life, the purpose of the Cosmos, is to gradually take form by evolving toward compassion and the fullness of love. To become love is the goal of evolution, so that at journey's end the Universe will be subsumed into love itself, be taken into the heart of God. All the pain and difficulties of this grand adventure are necessary, as are the visions of beauty and the ecstasies of joy. The Universe is one organic being, and we humans are a sublime expression of its life energy, the Cosmos become conscious. The task of each person in his or her life is to learn how to love. We learn this by embracing the kenotic nature of life, by choosing to move beyond the needs of the ego to give ourselves away. I believe this self-sacrifice is answered by a great promise; it is not futile or meaningless, as this kenosis leads to the homecoming of each individual and the whole Cosmos. Each act of self-donation is important. It is a movement into the life force that carries us toward love. What we choose to do every moment of every day is not lost because our efforts move the world away from death toward greater life. Each person is a player in a great drama, and there are no insignificant parts. Every individual is here to make a contribution, to actualize his or her potential to its limits, and to put the fruit of this effort at the service of love. No one can measure the significance of each life—the world is full of hidden heroes. I believe that the journey of the Cosmos through time has shape and meaning, and so I have tried to look at the questions that are the most fundamental to the human seeker: Where did we come from? What does life mean? Where are we going?

The centerpiece of *The Cosmic Pilgrim* is the new cosmology developed by the late Thomas Berry and his protégé Brian Swimme. A

Passionist priest, Berry was also a cultural historian and eco-theologian. He has been called the father of the new cosmology, but its grandfather must surely be Pierre Teilhard de Chardin who is the root thinker of this new vision. Swimme is a scientist, a mathematical cosmologist who seeks the integration of science with spirituality. The first section of this book, A New Story, is dedicated to capturing the main ideas of the new cosmology in order to provide a platform for further spiritual reflection. The question "Where did we come from?" is probed here. The second and third sections attempt to develop a spirituality based on some of the key principles of this worldview. Book 2, Cosmic Suffering, explores various answers to the pressing questions of why life is so difficult and painful, and why human beings have had such a difficult time living in harmony with the contours of existence. It looks at how they can better adapt to life in the Universe and become a healing, creative presence on planet Earth. This section roughly corresponds to the question "What does life mean?" Book 3, The Dream of God, tackles the "Where are we going?" subject. It probes a variety of responses to eschatological concerns ranging from thinkers who assert there is no afterlife to those who, like Teilhard de Chardin, believe the Cosmos is evolving toward a 'heavenly' future of fulfillment.

The perspective that I write from is something like deep ecology wedded with both science and Christianity. I draw on the Christian, Catholic tradition which has fed me all of my life because, although I am clearly a heretic, I believe that there are tremendously rich insights lying at the heart of Christianity that deserve preservation and attention despite the derision that often surrounds the word *Christian* in Western circles. I do not think that Christianity is necessarily the religion that resonates most closely with the new cosmology. In fact Buddhism and Taoism seem to be closer, but Christianity is what I know and love, and I would like to share its treasures. The fact that I try to write about scientific insights is laughable because I have always been an abysmal science student, and until I became fascinated with Brian Swimme's work, I had largely ignored the scientific world. I hope that knowledgeable readers will forgive my probable blunders in this regard.

Why did I write this book? The primary catalyst for putting pen to paper was to integrate my Christian beliefs with the exciting spirituality emerging from science. For years I had felt stagnant in my own spirituality and increasingly alienated from Christian doctrine. When I stumbled upon the new cosmology, I immediately felt that this was the way forward. These insights could provide a framework for the evolution of Christianity. I can certainly say that, through this creative exercise, I have discovered a new, more satisfying worldview and spirituality. Another pressing need I wished to address was the environmental crisis, which is not separate from the human crisis. I wanted to write a book that would give hope to my children as they face a very compromised future, something that would express my own core beliefs and perhaps act as an anchor for them as they move into adulthood. Lastly, I wanted to make my contribution to society by promoting the principles of the new cosmology. I wished to do my part in developing a spirituality that was pertinent for seekers of the twenty-first century.

In many ways, the human beings of this time, at least those in the western hemisphere, are lost in space. They have let go of the anchors that used to keep them from going adrift and are coping with life with stoic forbearance, focusing entirely on the delights of the present moment so that they do not have to peer into the darkness and emptiness that surrounds them on all sides. Ever since they discovered that the Sun does not move around the Earth, they have felt displaced and insignificant. They do not know where they came from or where they are going to. The wisdom of the day insists that religion is an immature and largely destructive response to the pressing need for ultimate meaning that insists on popping up unwanted. Although science can offer all the mystery and wonder that the heart needs in order to be thrilled and awed by existence, on its own it cannot provide a satisfying cosmology for the human race.

The Cosmic Pilgrim is about good news and hope. It attempts to convey a comprehensive and satisfying cosmology that is born of both scientific and religious visions. The foundational undercurrent of these personal offerings is the belief that neither science nor religion alone can steer a course to guide humans home to their ultimate destiny. For all its incredible discoveries and supreme intelligence, science is deliberately non-teleological. Its power lies in empirical data not spiritual supposition. Religion is rich in the distilled wisdom of human seekers reaching back into the mists of time, but it is mired in its particularism, its rigid doctrines, and dogmas that encase meaning in too stifling a space. The world needs a fresh wind to blow in from heaven and sweep away the old, dead leaves from the ground of religion and reveal the green shoots urgently pushing their way upward. I believe that the emerging cosmology this book explores offers the ideal ground for this new growth to thrive in. The story of the Universe in its wonder and mystery is a natural home for the meaning-making questions of religion: Where did all this come from? What does life mean? Where will the cosmic journey lead us? There are no complete answers to those questions because meaning itself is along for the ride, evolving with the rest of the whole show. We can only walk in the light that is present now, but as long as we have a glimmer of the profound meaning that lies at the heart of existence, we will no longer be lost in space. A new energy and joy will help us cope with the vicissitudes of life.

It is fashionable to say there are no answers to life's big questions, yet I think that an answer has been announcing its presence from every nook and cranny of the Universe since it exploded into the awareness of conscious creatures. We do not fully understand what it is yet, but primordial human beings sensed it from the beginning, and its resonance has continued intact through all subsequent generations. Augustine of Hippo described it as "a beauty ever ancient, ever new."[1] While knowledge and meaning have evolved and continue to broaden the horizons of our perception, this answer glows at the heart of things and grows brighter all the time: The Universe is held in being by love. Love is our source, our raison d'être, and our destination. We are not lost—we have always been found.

1. Augustine, *Confessions*, 10.27.

BOOK I

A New Story

One of the more remarkable achievements of the twentieth century is our ability to tell the story of the Universe from empirical observation and with amazing insight into the sequence of transformations that has brought into being the Earth, the living world, and the human community. There seems, however, to be little realization of just what this story means in terms of the larger interpretation of the human venture.[1]

[B]eyond physical and social needs, we have yet another need, one that is just as vital to our long-term health and happiness. It is a need that encompasses all the rest, an aspect of human life that is so mysterious it is often disregarded or denied. Like air and water, like the love and companionship of our kind, we need spiritual connection; we need to understand where we belong.[2]

HUMAN BEINGS LOVE STORIES. Perhaps this is so because we know there is more to life than our routine patterns. We are irresistibly drawn to mystery and the deeper purposes we sense below the surface of the mundane. Since ancient times, we have relied on stories to give shape and meaning to our tenuous existence on this magnificent and dangerous

1. Berry, *Dream of Earth*, xi.
2. Suzuki, *Sacred Balance*, 184.

1

planet within the swirling immensity of the Cosmos. All stories explore the meaning of life at some level, but there are overarching stories, called myths or grand narratives, that seek to convey answers to the fundamental human questions of where we came from, where we are going, and what life means. These are the stories that I am referring to in this chapter.

SACRED STORIES

Where do these epic stories come from? Over history they have emerged within human cultures reaching back to the most primitive forms of community. Before the rise of the great religions, myths were nature-centered, drawing purpose from the Earth's numinosity. With the dawn of religion, humans reached for connection with the transcendence that was blossoming within their expanding consciousness. Sacred stories carry the distilled wisdom and the collective longing of our ancestors in their quest for understanding and fulfillment. Some would say these stories are revealed from the divine realm, and the human storyteller is simply a recording instrument receiving dictation. Others would say they well up from the human imagination in response to the challenging mystery and wonder of life. Perhaps it is closer to the truth to say that these grand narratives come from both divine revelation and also from human questing for meaning within mystery.

Personally, I believe that the sacred stories of the world are human responses to divine encounters. I imagine people reaching up and God reaching down (forgive the dualist imagery), as in Michelangelo's *Creation of Adam*, and as their fingers touch, a story sparks into being. As humans yearn for understanding and fulfillment, so God longs to be known and met. The rest is Scripture. Sacred stories can never be fixed and normative for all time because divine revelation is ongoing, and developing human consciousness is ever more able to receive more of God's self-disclosure. The history of mythology tells the story of this expanding awareness.

Here in the West, we have lived for the past two thousand years or so mostly within the Christian grand narrative that goes something like this: The one God, who exists eternally beyond time and space, created the whole Universe, and within it the Earth. All that was created on Earth was very good until humans, who were formed from the soil, disrupted the original harmony by disobeying God who was the father of all. Creation then became chaotic and subject to time and death. Human beings continued to wreak havoc through their evil ways, and God as a loving parent continually forgave them and tried to teach them the right way to live through prophets and messengers. At last, God knew that the only way to repair the damage that had been caused by human disobedience was to send his only son, who would be a human being as well as God. This son, Jesus, was born into Earthly time and taught the people what God was really like, how to behave in a loving way, and how they could bring about the kind of world God wanted on Earth. Knowing that humans were incapable of doing this themselves, Jesus gave himself up to death to join human beings back to life in God. He reversed the separation caused by disobedience. God the father responded to Jesus' act of unconditional love by raising him from death, showing the human race that, if they joined themselves to Jesus, they too could live forever with God in heaven. After Jesus returned to live with the Father, he sent his Holy Spirit to live within all people who were open to receiving it, and this Spirit continued the work of Jesus on Earth. At the end of each life, people are judged by how well they have lived and then directed either to heaven to live eternally in joy with God, or to hell where God is eternally absent and human souls are forever in anguish. At the end of time, Jesus will come again to the Earth and close down the current realm of existence, bringing final judgment to human beings.

I was born into the Judeo-Christian cosmology, and it thrilled, comforted, and challenged me during my growing years and into adulthood. As an adult, I sought and found deeper insight into the tenets of my inherited religion. At some point, I stopped approaching it literally and became nourished by the profound symbolism behind every facet of the story. I can clearly remember the time when, in a high school religion lesson, I learned about the cosmology of the Hebrews from which the Bible emerged. I was startled and amazed to hear that the Genesis creation stories came from a worldview where the Earth was considered a flat plain, covered by a dome that separated the waters above from the waters below. This impressed upon my young mind that the Bible was far more than a history book and could not be relied on for its scientific accuracy. I gradually discovered that stories or myths carry layers of truth and meaning. I also came to realize, through studying the scriptures, that historical fact and symbolic mythology move freely in and out of each other, offering complementarity and different approaches to the story.

The great truths revealed by the world's religions are not fixed and absolute but plunge us ever deeper into mystery. I think that all the best stories take us down to the same fundamental truth that resonates with all people. Rather than thinking of religions as right or wrong, I see them as different jewels in a treasure chest—each one shining with its own color and radiance. I love the diamond of Christianity because I have learned over the years to appreciate the splendors it reflects; they have created a deep attraction and resonance in me. This is not to say that I do not also admire the sapphire of the Buddha or the ruby of the Tao. I believe that the ancient truth that shines from this treasure chest is evolving, always building on itself as time carries the Cosmos forward into ever-greater depth, unity and beauty. There is no need to look back at the past and say this or that belief was wrong and should be discarded; rather new knowledge includes and encompasses past understanding as horizons gradually expand.

Stories create cosmologies or worldviews. A story that conveys meaningful, satisfying answers to the fundamental human questions of where we came from, where we are going, and what life means, carries with it the power to form the way we think and, therefore, the way we act. We use words like philosophy, spirituality, or cosmology to describe our way of being in the world. Cosmology carries with it a sense of being situated within a universal horizon, and it is the word that will come up continually in this book because it carries the essence of the new story I want to talk about.[3]

Human societies have always been held together by their stories. The myths we live by are so ingrained and deeply rooted in our consciousness that they appear virtually invisible to us. They are simply the reality we live. Although these stories seem static and eternal to the generations of

3. On the one hand, cosmology is a distinct subset of physics. It is the exploration of the nature, origin and development of the Universe. As a scientist, Swimme studied and taught this, but he found it too limiting and dissatisfying. He wanted to explore the meaning and destiny of the Cosmos and, in particular, the meaning and destiny of human life within the Cosmos. Cosmology within this philosophical framework has a different definition. It refers to an ancient wisdom tradition that spans science, religion, art, and philosophy and allows for integration and synthesis. The phrase 'the new cosmology' when used by Brian Swimme and Thomas Berry refers to the encompassing story of the Universe from the fireball at the beginning of time, through the various stages of the emergence of life forms, through the development of the historic cultures of humankind, to present day realities and speculation about the future. It is an inter-disciplinary study based on empirical knowledge.

human beings who are guided by them, in fact they shift and evolve as new knowledge is gained and new horizons open up. Each major shift in a cosmology causes great turbulence and crisis as the old ideas die and new ones are born. New stories form from the creative sparks caused by the collision of new and old ideas. When we bump up against a different worldview, it is common for people to react defensively, rejecting this new interpretation of what life is about, but we might also feel intrigued, curious, and attracted. If we have been bothered for a while by certain aspects of our own belief system, finding them unsatisfying, confusing, or inadequate, we might try on a new worldview to see if it fits better with our personal quest for meaning. This is a good jumping off point for telling my own personal story of change and discovery.

MY STORY

I seem to be one of those people with a natural inclination toward religion. My personality, which leans heavily toward introverted, intuitive, reflective pondering, has always prodded me toward the central meaning-seeking questions of life. As a child, the all-embracing world of my parents' devout Catholicism provided rich ground for my questing spirit, and naturally enough, I would not have dreamed of questioning it during my formative years. I belonged securely to the Christian story, not only cerebrally but emotionally as well. I loved the garment of my family faith, which I wore enthusiastically.

The passing years brought minor crises of faith as my simple acceptance and understanding of Christianity gradually gave way to a certain skepticism and confusion about how well this view of things fit actual life. Some aspects of the Christian story bothered me deeply. I hated the notion that human beings had to take the blame for everything evil or painful in the world. In an effort to protect the image of an all-knowing, all-perfect, all-loving deity, it was deemed necessary to blame humans for anything that was perceived as wrong or imperfect. I wondered why so much suffering existed on Earth, and I rebelled against the answer that it was because human beings, in some primordial state, had messed up the perfection that God had intended for them by being disobedient. This view of things not only made humans look bad, but also made God look like a pathetic simpleton who did not know what he was doing creating these willful children with a mind of their own. The idea of God being an offended, yet long-suffering, parent who was always surprised when his children did yet another bad thing was quite ridiculous to me. Following from this, the whole sin and redemption framework gradually collapsed. The idea of the father God having to send his son to die a painful death in order to make things perfect again really made no sense to me. I suspected the death and resurrection of Jesus was more revelatory than redemptive, revealing the path toward salvation rather than achieving it once and for all. This is not the place to catalogue my growing dissatisfaction with the Christian cosmology, so I will simply say that I eventually reached a place where I had to empty myself of doctrine and dogma. I could no longer read the Bible, even though I wanted to, because it was too familiar to me within a cosmology that was no longer meaningful to me. I had to abstain for a long time before I could see Scripture with new eyes.

I came across the ideas of the new cosmology when I was empty, and they provided me with a new context within which to explore the treasures of my faith. I was in a place where I simply knew that God was, and I was in relationship with God. I knew nothing else. Then I allowed the new ideas to slowly seep into me. I felt as if I was a pupa hanging in my casing. Slowly, the skin of the old cosmology, which had been too tight for me, gradually split open, and a new vision of reality emerged within me. I have no wish to attack or destroy Christianity. Rather, the metamorphosis of the last ten years has directed me deep down into my old roots to re-imagine the treasures of Christianity within a new cosmology. This experience has been like the unfolding of something ancient-new. Slowly but surely, I am returning to the core beliefs of my religion and rediscovering them in a new way.

So why do we need a new sacred story? I believe that religion is struggling today under the burden of a cosmology that is antiquated and is inadequate to carry the vision needed for an understanding of the future of humankind and, indeed, the future of the Cosmos. Science has revealed to us an overarching epic within which the world's religions could find a rich and satisfying home. The profound insights of religious stories wedded with the scientific account of the nature of the Universe could be immensely fruitful in finding a new grand narrative for the human race. Within the unity of the epic of the Universe, the diversity of cultural and religious stories could find a new home.

My own tale of transformation speaks of the need to break out of a restrictive religious worldview. Brian Swimme's story tells of the need to break open an equally stifling scientific worldview. At this time in its history, Western culture has largely moved away from the sacred story that has shaped it over the last two thousand years and has embraced a secular story. It has taken science as its only reference, and science is not designed to provide a comprehensive worldview fit for accommodating the questing human spirit. Although this myth has freed the Western mind from an excessive otherworldliness and focused attention on the present moment, it has turned away from the ultimate meaning-making questions that give depth and purpose to life.

THE STORY OF SCIENCE

Science itself is entirely empirical and non-teleological—it simply does not ask meaning questions. In moving away from Christian cosmology, Western culture has largely embraced science as its fundamental frame of reference. It prides itself on just dealing with the facts and having no need of a grand narrative to provide meaning, but, of course, there always is a story lurking somewhere. Within science it is called scientism or scientific materialism and goes something like this: The scientific method is the only mode of finding out the truth about the world and how reality operates. Therefore, philosophical or religious claims are unnecessary and unreliable. Rather than recognizing that there are many ways of knowing, scientism asserts that there is only one way, that of science, and all the rest is nonsense. There is no such thing as the supernatural because it cannot be tested, and there is no purpose in natural things. Life does not mean anything in particular—it just is. The development of the Universe operates solely on the principle of chance, and there is no directionality in it. When all is said and done, only science can give access to reality as it is.

BRIAN'S STORY

I do not mean to suggest that all scientists approach reality from this perspective; indeed that is far from the truth. Many renowned scientists recognize that there are other ways of understanding life, and they balance their own perception with these. However, in the field of education, science professors are certainly expected to teach only the facts, and it is considered completely inappropriate to bring up questions of meaning in a science class. This is what caused great distress to Brian Swimme. In a way, he should have been pretty happy with the way his life was going. Finishing a PhD in gravitational physics, he acquired a teaching post at the University of Puget Sound in Tacoma, Washington, and his career as a bright, talented scientist was well on its way to success. And yet, despite all this and his happy family life, Brian was deeply disturbed and sorrowful about his job and about what he saw happening to the planet he so cherished. It became increasingly painful for him to teach about the Cosmos without connecting the facts with the meaning they seemed to point to. Being a natural mystic, he longed to discuss the story behind the phenomena. He also recognized the intimate connection between the mechanistic philosophy of scientism and the ecological disaster visiting the entire Earth. Viewing the diverse planetary life forms as objects to be manipulated—rather than as subjects to be respected—was producing devastating results, and Brian saw the desperate need for a new story that would help the human population understand the damage they were causing and provide ways of healing the Earth.

In a state of depression, he left his job and went on a quest to find a new direction for his life that would not only satisfy his questions about the meaning of the Universe, but also give him the opportunity to work toward a new way of relating to the Earth. He asked everyone he knew who would be the best person to show him a way forward, and the name of Thomas Berry kept coming up as humanity's best hope for a new vision. Leaving behind his old life, Brian moved with his family to New York so that Berry could become his mentor.

The next few years were, to use one of Brian's favorite words, a "shattering." Under Berry's tutelage, Brian took on an in-depth study of paleontologist/theologian Teilhard de Chardin and Berry's own work on the environment and cultural anthropology. Brian was able to bring his scientific knowledge to add to the mix, and out of this cauldron of creativity, a story emerged that goes something like this:

THE STORY OF THE UNIVERSE

To speak of the Universe's origin is to bring to mind the great silent fire at the beginning of time. This was a fire that filled the Universe—that was the Universe. There was no place in the Universe free from it. Every point of the Cosmos was a point of this explosion of light. And all the particles of the Universe churned in extremes of heat and pressure, all that we see about us, all that now exists was there at the beginning, in that great burning explosion of light . . . We can see the light from the primeval fireball. Or at least the light from its edge, for it burned for nearly a million years. We can see the dawn of the Universe because the light from its edge reaches us only now, after traveling twenty billion years to get here . . . It took millions of years to develop, but humans can now interact with the cosmic radiation from the origin of the Universe . . . Most amazing is the realization that every thing that exists in the Universe came from a common origin. The material of our bodies emerged from and is caught up in a single energetic event. Our ancestry stretches back through the life forms and into the stars, back to the beginnings of the primeval fireball. This Universe is a single multiform energetic unfolding of matter, mind, intelligence, and life . . . We are the first generation to live with an empirical view of the origin of the Universe. We are the first humans to look into the night sky and see the birth of stars, the birth of galaxies, the birth of the Cosmos as a whole. Our future as a species will be forged within this new story of the world . . . All that exists on Earth exists only through the elementary particles that emerged in that first epoch of the Universe's unfolding . . . We must realize that the creation of a galaxy is one stupendous activity . . . yet galaxies were created by the hundred billion, each with its hundred billion stars . . . And these stupendously complex systems of being simply leapt into existence. When we reflect on the creativity inherent in the Universe, we are overwhelmed both by its enormity and by its seeming effortlessness. To learn about creativity, we must begin to understand the creativity of the Earth. We know of no other planet with Earth's creative power . . . Earth was a cauldron of chemical and elemental creativity, fashioning ever more complex forms and combinations until life burst forth in the oceans and spread across the continents, covering the entire planet. This creativity advanced until flowers bloomed on every continent, then advanced further until the vision of the flowers and all beauty could be deeply felt and appreciated. We are the latest, the most recent, the youngest extravagance of this stupendously creative Earth . . . We are only just starting out on the human venture . . . the human self-reflexive mind continues to unfold . . . The Universe continues to unfold, continues to reveal itself to itself through human awareness . . . The human provides the space in which the Universe feels its stupendous beauty . . . We enable some of the depths of the Universe to be tasted, and we have only just begun our venture; much waits on our maturity . . . The Universe shivers with wonder in the depths of the human . . . [h]umans can house the tremendous beauty of Earth, of life, of the Universe. We can value it, feel its grandeur.

Each of the three eras of humanity has achieved its own unique vision of beauty. During the tribal-shamanic age, the great

mysteries of Earth and sky and Sun burst into human consciousness . . . Whenever we are moved to awe by the branching fire
of lightning, whenever we tremble with expectation in the pre-
dawn forest, we are remembering the Earth's first taste of its own
beauty.

In the second era of human history, that of the great classical civilizations, we witness the rise of the Chinese, the Indian,
the European, the Middle Eastern, the Amerindian. By enabling
humans to specialize in their work, civilizations brought forth human powers unimagined in the tribal world. In this matrix the
great scriptures of the world were written, the classical spiritual
disciplines forged. During this period of human history, there developed an appreciation for the human world as the intersection of
the transphenomenal and phenomenal realms.

The scientific-technological era is humanity's third phase of
development. In these last few centuries we have empirically pen-
etrated the dynamics governing the Earth and the Cosmos. The
gravitational, the electromagnetic, the weak and strong nuclear
interactions were discovered and encoded in mathematical language. The power to alter the Earth's dynamics through techno-
logical inventions was seized. The immensity of time and space
dawned within human awareness, and even the origins of the
Universe burst into the individual, self-reflexive awareness. The
scientific-technological period has enabled the dynamics of the
Universe to unfold in human consciousness.

At present, the human species moves into its fourth era, what
we might call the age of the Earth. This does not mean that science or technology will evaporate. The tribal-shamanic era did not
disappear when classical religious civilizations emerged, nor did
these civilizations all disappear when the scientific-technological
era began. But the creative fire within the human venture now
focuses on bringing forth something entirely new, a form of human life that envisions itself within the interconnected dynamics
of the unfolding Earth reality. The tribe will not be the center of
the human world, nor will the civilization, the culture, nor the na-
tion-state. It will be the Earth community as a whole that will be
understood as our home, our womb of creativity and life.

The creation story unfurling within the scientific enterprise provides the fundamental context, the fundamental arena
of meaning, for all the peoples of the Earth. For the first time in
human history, we can agree on the basic story of the galaxies,
the stars, the planets, minerals, life forms, and human cultures.
This story does not diminish the spiritual traditions of the classical or tribal periods of human history. Rather, the story provides

the proper setting for the teachings of all traditions, showing the true magnitude of their central truths. We are forging a cosmology that embraces humanity as a species, one that does not ignore the special cultural contributions of each continent, but that enhances these differences. Each tradition is irreplaceable. Not one can be reduced to any other. Each is vital to the work of the future. Each will flower beyond telling in the fruitful interaction with the rest in the overall embracing story of the Cosmos.[4]

Berry and Swimme propose this epic as an overarching story for the human race, not intended to debunk or replace all our other stories of religion and philosophy, but to provide an ultimate backdrop within which each individual story can take on a more universal cosmology or worldview. The Universe itself is a story. It is the grand narrative out of which the new human story will emerge. This is not simply the story of matter coming into existence and then spreading out and forming a gigantic, deterministic, material Cosmos; it is more like the story of an emergent being. To understand it means letting go of previous categories and becoming open to a radically new way of seeing reality. This story had a beginning, we are all caught up in its unfolding, and it will have an end, which may be part of a new beginning for everything we know. Science has given us knowledge about the birth and unfolding of the Universe and continues to amaze us with incredible discoveries about the nature of reality. However, science alone cannot tell the story properly because it is too limited by its own agenda. It is superbly designed to give us the facts, but it is not equipped to talk about what these facts mean. In order to really penetrate the stupendous mystery of the Cosmos in a multi-dimensional way that can provide a whole worldview, we need religion, philosophy, art, and all the collective wisdom that humans have amassed over the ages. The new story does not replace old stories but invites them to evolve in a new way.

This then is the skeleton of the new story, the new cosmology, and its implications for a new way of being in the world are numerous. We will need guides to help us understand them. Although many thinkers will be drawn upon to enflesh this new vision of reality, our chief guides will be Brian Swimme, Thomas Berry, and Teilhard de Chardin. The chapters in book 1 are roughly based on what Berry calls principles of a functional cosmology.

4. Swimme, *Universe is Green Dragon*, 27–39.

The Universe is the Primary Revelation of God

To SAY THAT THE Universe itself is revelatory is a profound leap away from both scientific materialism, which sees no numinous meaning behind the facts of cosmic properties, and revealed religion, which sees sacred Scripture as the prime source of revelation and the Cosmos as a kind of stage where this occurs. In light of this, the central principle of the new cosmology appears as controversial: "The Universe, the solar system, and the planet Earth in themselves and in their evolutionary emergence constitute for the human community the primary revelation of that ultimate mystery whence all things emerge into being."[1] In an interview with *U.S. Catholic* magazine, Swimme, in a rare religious comment, describes the Universe as the foremost means of knowing God: "In the spirit of Aquinas, I would say that the Universe itself is the primary revelation of God, and the Universe is made in the image and likeness of God."[2]

FROM DUALISM TO HOLISM

When I was first introduced to this principle, and the implications of it began to sink in for me, it seemed as if I had come across a crucial piece of a puzzle I had been trying to assemble for a long time. Throughout my spiritual life to this point, I had felt an uncomfortable sense of dualism between religion and the actual concrete reality of my experience. Even though I had internalized the belief that God was present in everything—a belief that, after all, is common and ordinary to Christianity—the underlying message I was hearing from within my religious world was that the most important knowledge about God was only to be found in the Bible and teachings of the church, and that, in some sense, I had to withdraw

1. Swimme, *Canticle to Cosmos*, 1.
2. U.S. Catholic Eds, "Where does your faith."

from everyday experience to find God. The Cosmos was like a backdrop to all that, not a main player. Over the years, I felt a growing hunger for a more radically incarnational faith—more real in terms of human experience within the surrounding world.

Of course, I was not alone in experiencing this duality as it arises from a common philosophical heritage in Western society. Despite the movement into postmodernism that has challenged all the old dualities, the West, and particularly Western religion, still has one foot in the past and continues to endorse the infamous split between matter and spirit. The belief that brute matter is separate from and infinitely inferior to noetic and spiritual realities is a hard one to shake. The new cosmology has helped me to make the leap into a more holistic and unified spirituality.

Everything that exists now had an identical source within the fireball at the beginning of time. That is not a controversial statement at first glance because we have become used to acknowledging that our bodies, along with all life forms, rocks and minerals, etc., emerged from the same building blocks that were present in the original fireball. However, we are not so used to the idea that religion, music, poetry, all types of creativity, and our very soul is a gift of the Universe. Of course, it took billions of years for all these to emerge to their current state, but the central point is that what we consider matter is not something separate from spirit—it is all one seamless garment. The more scientists look for the most basic form of matter, the more it eludes them. Quantum physics has shown us that even the most solid-looking block of matter is actually better described as energy; indeed, nothing is as it seems. The primal energy that gave birth to all that we know (and don't know) is 'bio-spiritual.' Swimme contends that there is no energy in the Universes that is not. Despite its complexity and depth, Shakespeare's *Hamlet* is a further explicitation of the basic stuff of existence.

TEILHARD'S NEW VISION OF THE SACRED

As Pierre Teilhard de Chardin (1881–1955) is a central thinker to this book, it is time to introduce him. He was a French Roman Catholic priest belonging to the Jesuit order, and he was also a scientist—a paleontologist who studied the fossils of prehistoric ages. Teilhard became fascinated with the integration of his scientific insights about evolution and the nature of matter with his religious beliefs. He lived and wrote at a time when the Christian church was experiencing the new science, particularly in its evolutionary aspects, as a threat to its own integrity. For the most part, the Roman Catholic Church reacted defensively to this new knowledge, on the one hand reiterating the unchangeable nature of its own doctrines, and on the other hand silencing any voice of dissent. The revolutionary ideas of Teilhard were not well received. He was not permitted to publish any of his works or speak publicly on theological matters.

Teilhard saw himself as a loyal member of the Catholic Church and hoped that his work might help to integrate science and Christianity. He tried to "reconstruct the most basic Christian doctrines from the perspectives of science, and, at the same time, to reconstruct science from the perspectives of faith."[3] His vision of a unified reality made it impossible for him to divide the world up between science and religion, and he saw that the only way to move forward was to integrate the two: "After close on two centuries of passionate struggles, neither science nor faith has succeeded in discrediting its adversary. On the contrary, it becomes obvious that neither can develop normally without the other. And the reason is simple: the same life animates both. Neither in its impetus nor its achievements can science go to its limits without becoming tinged with mysticism and charged with faith."[4]

Learning how to see the world in both a concrete and numinous way was all-important to Teilhard. He said the "history of the living world can be summarized as the elaboration of ever more perfect eyes within a Cosmos in which there is always something more to be seen."[5] Part of this 'seeing' was the gift of science, teaching religion to take notice of and take seriously the physical world; part of it was the gift of religion, teaching science to see the sacred dimension of all creation.

Teilhard challenged both the worlds of religion and science and, tragically, was marginalized by both. The Catholic Church was not receptive to being instructed in this manner. He was silenced and banished from France to China, yet his friends disseminated his ideas informally. His works, written over a period from 1924 to 1955, were only published after his death. Although a respected scientist within the field of paleontology, Teilhard's religious views were not welcome within the scientific

3. Henderson, *God and Science,* chap. 5, para. 1.

4. Teilhard de Chardin, *Phenomenon of Man,* 311.

5. Ibid., 35.

community. Today, he gets mixed reviews from the worlds of science and religion, but enthusiastic disciples from both disciplines continue to probe his ideas and find ongoing relevance for the current science/religion dialogue.

Central to Teilhard's cosmology was the assertion that the material world is revelatory of the divine. For him there was no duality between the sacred and the profane, for everything in creation radiated the divine: "Everything glows, expands, is impregnated with . . . the Absolute. Even more, everything is animated with a flow of Presence and of Love."[6] Teilhard saw the humblest detail of life as revelatory. He asserted that the material world of rocks, plants, and animals was not simply the stuff of scientific exploration but was the source of "a new vision of the holy. The very subject matter of pure science was nothing less than a mirror in which one could see reflected the face of God."[7] Teilhard proposed that everything in the Universe, even the most elemental material substance has an inside and an outside, a 'within' and a 'without.' The *without* of matter is its physical nature and appearance, which is empirically measurable and readily acceptable to science, but Teilhard argued that science was avoiding acknowledging the *within* of matter by restricting consciousness to human beings. The within is the consciousness, the psychic and spiritual dimension of matter which exists in an obvious way in human beings, but which is harder to discern the further back in evolution one travels, until it is only discernible in latent or embryonic form.[8] This insistence on the inner dimension of matter is at the heart of Teilhard's vision and was an extraordinary idea in his time. Swimme recognizes him as one of the first thinkers to see the Universe as having a spiritual as well as a physical dimension: "He began to see the universe in an integral way, not as just objective matter but as suffused with psychic or spiritual energy."[9] The Cosmos is a "cosmogenesis," one unfolding unity of all that is, a process where consciousness is on the rise. In his characteristically succinct style, Swimme says, "This Universe is a single multiform energetic unfolding of matter, mind, intelligence, and life."[10]

---

6. Teilhard de Chardin, *Future of Mankind,* chap. 3, sec. 5.

7. Henderson, *God and Science,* chap. 5, para. 10.

8. Teilhard de Chardin, *Phenomenon of Man,* 58–72.

9. Bridle, "Divinization of Cosmos."

10. Swimme, *Universe is Green Dragon,* 28.

Teilhard proposed that there is a progressive development to the evolution of the Universe. It is on a journey to a more highly conscious form. He perceived within nature a pattern, which he named the cosmic law of complexity-consciousness.[11] Over the course of our planet Earth's evolution, very simple forms, which had a low level of both complexity and consciousness, joined together to become more complex forms, which then became more conscious. The more complex forms became, the more conscious they became. Teilhard scholar Beatrice Bruteau describes this law occurring at all levels of evolution: "More complex and more conscious beings are formed by the union of less complex and less conscious elements with one another. Subatomic particles unite to form atoms, atoms unite to form molecules, molecules unite to form cells, and cells unite to form organisms. This same pattern of creating something new, something more complex and more conscious, by the union of the less complex and less conscious recurs at each of these levels."[12]

Therefore, consciousness or spirit (in this context, I am using these as synonyms) gradually emerged in the Universe through forms becoming more and more complex. In human beings, consciousness took on a new expansiveness. Human self-reflexive consciousness, with its amazing depth and sensitivity, was born from the simpler level of animal consciousness. According to Teilhard, the future holds a continuing evolution of human consciousness to a level that is more global yet unified, more sensitive to beauty and goodness, more characterized by love, until finally a critical mass of complexity-consciousness is reached and love is all in all. For Teilhard the aim of the Universe is to become love. (But I am getting too far ahead of myself. The scope of Teilhard's vision will, hopefully, emerge before this book is finished.)

GEO-BIO-SPIRITUALITY

Swimme makes the startling statement that if the rocks are not spiritual, then we are not spiritual. All things exist within their own consciousness or latent consciousness—something we have only attributed to humans in the past. The rocks themselves are our ancestors within an evolutionary perspective and have their own presence and power. A sensitive human being can experience their numinous quality: "Stones to me are just suf-

11. Teilhard de Chardin, *Phenomenon of Man*, 328.

12. Edelstein and Daly, "A Song."

fusing the world with radiance, sometimes it's unbearable, it's a shattering to approach a stone."[13] The Universe is not just a huge amount of empty space interspersed with inert matter within which a few conscious and even fewer reflexive-conscious beings exist. It is a unity—a unified material, spiritual organism. We humans are the Universe become conscious of itself in a particular way.

It becomes possible to begin to understand how the Universe is the primary revelation of God. This way of thinking decentralizes human beings from their privileged position as the sole arena for revelation. Revelation involves the whole Cosmos: the entire planetary, cosmic community is needed to understand who God is. Within this spirituality, the concept of God becomes more mysterious, less nameable, and more awesome than in the familiar world of religious revelation, yet there is no fundamental contradiction between the God revealed by the Cosmos and the God revealed within the world's great religions. Swimme and Berry do not generally use the word *God* but usually speak of 'ultimate mystery' or 'ultimate reality.' They do this because they believe that the word *God* has a tendency to truncate any concept of divinity. Religions have sometimes used it to naively personify, domesticate, and limit the divine. Swimme and Berry wish to avoid that trap. I use the word *God* throughout this book for the sake of simplicity, to honor its use by generations before us, and to draw it into a more cosmic, evolutionary context. However, I see this word as a metaphor for the embracing, life-giving love in which the Universe has its being, and which the Universe is becoming.

This then is the foundational statement for the new cosmology—that the Universe in its sheer existence and in its evolutionary pattern is the primary revelation of the divine. The Universe in itself and also in its evolutionary mode is revelatory. The fact that we evolve is itself an amazing fact. Understanding time in this fashion has been, perhaps, the single most important insight of the last century. We now know that our individual lives are part of a cosmic story, on a journey from a beginning to an end. This raises vital questions about the meaning and purpose of life: Where did we come from? Where are we going? What does life ask of us? How are we to understand human life in the context of a vast, unfolding Universe? How does God fit into all this? These are the questions that we will explore in this book.

13. Swimme, *Canticle to Cosmos*, 1.

GOD'S SELF-COMMUNICATION TO CREATION

The idea that the Universe is the primary revelation of God is a problematic claim for those of us within the Christian tradition, because we have always associated this with our Scriptures and traditions, which we believe reveal the nature and desire of God. We see them as God's self-revelation. They capture the communication of God to human beings—they are the Word of God. I am not talking here about some crude dictation of divine intent to a mere recorder, but of the experience of humans-being-in-relation to God. The sacred Scriptures did not drop from heaven. They are the stories of the human quest for the sacred, the unfolding of the realization of who God is, a recognition that an invitation has been given—a relationship offered.

How can religious theophany be considered in relation to the Universe being the primary revelation of God? I do not think that there is any need for competition between the two because revelation is all of one piece. God has been revealing the divine nature and will from the first moment of time, and the Cosmos has received this revelation to the extent it was able over the eons. The revelation of religion is a further explicitation of divine communication—as consciousness develops, so does the world's capacity to receive and understand it. Humankind, with its incredible gift of self-reflexive consciousness, is a further expression of the Universe itself awakening to an ever-deepening knowledge of God. Religious revelation must be seen within this context, as a further evolution of a knowledge that was seeded in the Earth from its conception. It cannot be separated from its origins without perverting the clarity and depth of its true meaning. It is the evolutionary perspective that characterizes the power of this insight. The realization that the Universe is evolving has changed forever the way human beings look at everything—even God.

Before the era of the great world religions, the revelation of God shone clearly from the natural world. Since the inauguration of religion, the sacred vision has been articulated in a way that has gradually become an entity of its own, separate from the Universe and the world of experience and sometimes hostile to it and fearful of it. This world is too small. Religion is groping forward towards its next evolutionary stage. It does not need to lose all that it has gained over the last several thousand years, but it needs a wider vision. Life is always groping forward, and religion, as part of it, is groping also. We live in interesting times.

This primary principle of the new cosmology suggests that the sacred Scriptures and religious doctrines honored by Christianity and all the religions of the Earth are derivative. They came from and exist within the wider context of the Universe story. However, this in no way makes them second best. They are a further phase of the unfolding of God's self-communication to creation and are absolutely essential to the ongoing evolution of revelation. It is possible that at this time the era of the great religions is passing as something new is born. If this is so, it is imperative that their treasures should not be lost, but find their place within the framework of a revelation that began at the dawn of time. Nothing worthy is lost by the Universe because the experiences of the past are the building blocks of the future. The fiery glow at the heart of religion can never be extinguished but will flare up brighter than ever within the contours of a wider cosmology: "This story does not diminish the spiritual traditions of the classical or tribal periods of the human story. Rather, the story provides the proper setting for the teachings of all traditions, showing the true magnitude of the central truths."[14] And again Swimme tells us, "Each tradition is irreplaceable. Not one can be reduced to any other. Each is vital to the work of the future. Each will flower beyond telling in the fruitful interaction with the rest of the overall embracing story of the Cosmos."[15] The Universe is the primary revelation of God because it is the primary all-pervading context for all revelation.

14. Swimme, *Universe is Green Dragon*, 37.
15. Ibid., 39.

2

The Source of the Universe

ACCORDING TO BRIAN SWIMME, the desire to know our origins is at
least as strong as our desire for water. We long to know where we
came from. Science can take us back to the origins of the Universe and
inform us that our current state of existence is the culmination of the epic
journey, through vast stretches of time, of the original building materials
of the Universe. Everything that exists now, including human consciousness, was present in latent form at the beginning, in the flaring forth of the
Universe. But then we enter the realm of mystery, where all science can do
is give indications of where the whole Universe came from, of what happened before the Big Bang. Physics cannot, and should not be expected
to, draw any teleological conclusions from the data it has gathered using
the scientific method. However, it is next to impossible for human beings
to leave it at that. We want to know where everything came from and
what this can tell us about the meaning of existence itself.

NOWHERE, NOTHINGNESS, AND EMPTINESS

One of the indications that could point to the origins of the Universe
comes from the little understood field of quantum theory. Quantum
physicists have discovered an inexplicable and strange occurrence known
as quantum fluctuation. They have been amazed to discover, within a
vacuum where all elements known to us are removed, particles appear-
ing out of nowhere: "Even where there are no atoms, and no elementary
particles, and no protons, and no photons, suddenly elementary particles
will emerge."[1] Can quantum fluctuation tell us anything about the birth
of the Universe? It seems to point to a mysterious realm from which everything emerged. For Swimme it means that "being, itself ar[ose] out

1. Swimme, *Hidden Heart,* 92.

of a field of fecund emptiness . . . it simply leapt out of no-thing-ness."[2] Not only do particles suddenly appear in quantum fluctuation, they just as mysteriously disappear again. Where did they come from? Where are they going?

The words nothingness and emptiness need some explanation here. Neither science nor religion proposes that there is really any such thing as true emptiness—literally a space or entity of non-existence. Both speak of emptiness as being a realm unavailable to human exploration, which is actually teeming with a fullness we cannot grasp or understand. Swimme speaks of "an empty realm, a mysterious order of reality, a no-thing-ness that is simultaneously the ultimate source of all things."[3] We use the word *empty* because of the limitations of human language and conceptualization. But this emptiness is fuller than we can imagine. It is a nothing that is everything. From this nothing all things come into being. In religious terms, Swimme describes the birth of the Universe as the "great eruption out of the Godhead," fifteen billion years ago.[4]

What can be said spiritually about this empty realm? Swimme proposes that it is the source of all creativity. All that is emerges from it and also returns to it when the journey in space-time is over. All that is born returns to its source. He describes it as an "all-nourishing abyss,"[5] choosing his words carefully to indicate a dual emphasis: "the Universe's generative potentiality is indicated with the phrase 'all-nourishing,' but the Universe's power of infinite absorption is indicated with 'abyss.'"[6] It is not a thing or a physical place so much as "a power that gives birth and that absorbs existence at a thing's annihilation."[7] This is consistent with religious revelation, whether it posits reincarnation or a linear pathway to eternity. All creation arises from the Godhead and returns to it when the Earthly journey (or journeys in the case of reincarnation) is over.

Even though the Universe erupted from this mysterious, bountiful source fifteen billion years ago, this does not mean that emergence is an event in the past. Creation is ongoing—it still happens at every moment.

2. Swimme, *Universe is Green Dragon*, 93.

3. Ibid., 36.

4. U.S. Catholic Eds., "Where does your faith."

5. Swimme, *Hidden Heart,* 100.

6. Ibid., 100.

7. Ibid., 100.

Protons and antiprotons are flashing in and out of existence all the time and everywhere. The power of creativity is within each instant of the past, present, and future. The Universe is continually surging into existence—a continuing birth—each new face, each new moment is part of this birth. We see here the contingent nature of reality. All things are held in being by the persistent, abundant power from which the Universe emerged.

This fertile emptiness is not just in outer space or in an originating realm beyond the Universe; it is within all things—it is within each one of us. Swimme tell us, "This plenary emptiness permeates you. You are more fecund emptiness than you are created particles . . . Indeed, if all the space were taken out of you, you would be a million times smaller than the smallest grain of sand."[8] Each atom is a tiny amount of matter and mostly emptiness. The so-called empty space of the Universe is both a creative womb and a numinous presence that pervades and sustains all existence. Swimme comes close to describing what Christian theology would call the Holy Spirit. The originating power is "protean, untiring, confident, enflamed, unitive, irresistible."[9] It permeates the Universe and our own selves.

THE FORMLESS PATH

The connection of emptiness to Eastern religions is fairly apparent, and several scholars have attempted to explore the relationship between quantum physics and the spirituality of the East. Gary Zukav, in his book *The Dancing Wu Li Masters*, speaks of Eastern religions being "based upon the experience of a pure, undifferentiated reality which is that-which-is."[10] The language that physicists have available to them to describe the effects they observe is clearly inadequate because, as Zukav points out, language is a system of symbols based upon the rules of classical logic. The quantum world has its own logic, resting on experience rather than symbols. Thus, quantum physicists sound exactly like Buddhist monks when they try to verbalize the indescribable world of pure experience: "Everything is a manifestation of that which is. That which is, is. Beyond these words lies the experience; the experience of that which is."[11] Professor David Bohm

8. Swimme, *Universe is Green Dragon*, 37–38.

9. Ibid., 64.

10. Zukav, *Dancing Wu Li Masters*, 322.

11. Ibid., 297.

tries to explain the difficulties in comprehending the nature of reality: "Reality means 'everything you can think about.' This is not 'that which is.' No idea can capture 'truth' in the sense of that-which-is."[12]

Zukav believes that science is coming to an end in terms of the way it has proceeded so far. He sees that in coming face to face with the ineffable, science must lead Western civilization "in its own time and in its own way, into the higher dimensions of human experience . . . We need not make a pilgrimage to India or Tibet. There is much to learn there, but here at home, in the most inconceivable of places, amidst the particle accelerators and computers, our own Path without Form is emerging."[13] Perhaps the future of science is a kind of mysticism. In fact, it is not unimaginable that, in the future, mysticism may be the meeting place of science and religion. As both disciplines follow the path of knowledge to its departure into mystery, perhaps they will together be able to let go of their dogmas and unite under the umbrella of 'not knowing.'

Fritjof Capra is famous for his insights into the connection between physics and Eastern religions. In *The Tao of Physics* he says, "In the Eastern view, the reality underlying all phenomena is beyond all forms and defies all description and specification. It is therefore often said to be formless, empty or void. But this emptiness is not to be taken for mere nothingness. It is, on the contrary, the essence of all forms and the source of all life."[14] In Buddhism, the ultimate reality is called *Sunyata*, which means emptiness, or the void. It gives birth to all existing phenomena. Taoists call this creative void the Tao. Capra goes on to compare the emptiness of Eastern mysticism to the quantum field of subatomic physics: "Like the quantum field, it gives birth to an infinite variety of forms which it sustains and, eventually, reabsorbs."[15] Just as subatomic particles move in and out of existence, so the phenomena of creation arise from the void and return to it once again in due course.

NON-BEING AND THE WEST

Western thought has also intuited that emptiness is the source of everything, although this is not evident until one looks into the mystical stream

12. Ibid., 323.

13. Ibid., 327.

14. Capra, *Tao of Physics*, 211.

15. Ibid., 212.

that flows virtually hidden at the core of Christianity. Great mystics such as Meister Eckhart spoke of the creative void in their own conceptual language. Eckhart understood this realm of the not-put-together as the ultimate simplicity of the Godhead. Perhaps Teilhard de Chardin would be the best spokesperson for Christian mysticism in this context. His thought is very complex and sometimes quite obscure, but it reveals a profound resonance with the same mystery of being and non-being that we have seen in Eastern mysticism.

Teilhard was drawn to matter, or something that he sensed as radiating from the core of matter, from an early age. Upon pondering the seeming permanence and yet impermanence of material things, he came to realize that matter is nothing of itself, but only a reflection of the true being from which it arose, and to which it is destined to return after its transformative journey to oneness with God. The radiance he saw in matter was the reflected glory of God because material things of themselves are only transient and in process. He was developing his ideas at the same time that physicists were entering the astonishing world of quantum theory. He saw fellow scientists seeking to grasp the basic form of matter from which the Universe is made, peering ever deeper into the micro world of the smallest particles, only to find their probing halted as matter disappeared into the mystery of emptiness. Teilhard drew his own paradoxical conclusions from this extraordinary discovery. As Thomas King, an eminent Teilhard scholar, describes them, "Matter is the non-being that is; it only reflects."[16] Matter of itself is process and impermanence and has no real being; therefore, "it is only the reflector of Being it does not possess; in itself matter has no real unity, it is only the reflector of a unity it does not possess."[17] Matter is the alluring mirror that reflects the ultimate reality that is God.

As a loyal follower of Christian metaphysics, Teilhard did not come to the monistic conclusion that all reality is an undifferentiated oneness, but his commonality with Eastern religions lay in his intuitive understanding that matter itself is emptiness. He believed that it was necessary to plunge into this emptiness in order to discover the God who draws the Cosmos upwards toward the fullness of being. For Teilhard, direct experience of the world is essential to understanding God. Science offers a way

16. King, *Teilhard's Mysticism*, 30.
17. Ibid., 30.

of descending into matter and discovering the true nature of existence. He suggested that physicists are offered the possibility of becoming true mystics.[18] True to his roots in Teilhardian philosophy, Swimme speaks of the non-visible reality that shows itself in time within the journey toward eternal fullness: "The true significance of the discovery of the quantum vacuum is the new understanding it provides concerning the reality of the nonvisible. Time is not the fullness of being. There is existence and there is emptiness. Both are real. The eternal, the trans-phenomenal, shows itself in time, yes, just as the dynamics of the Cosmos show themselves in concrete events. But what is invisible is real as well."[19]

18. Ibid., 111.
19. Swimme, *Hidden Heart*, 97.

3

Allurement, Love, and Comprehensive Compassion

FOLLOWING IN THE TRADITION of Teilhard de Chardin, and indeed the whole mystic tradition, Brian Swimme asserts that the power that gave birth to the Universe, and continues to sustain it, is love. He takes this up and demonstrates that the physical laws of the Universe are revelatory of the basic nature of love. It is reflected in all aspects of existence. Even gravity, which holds the Universe together, is a primitive form of love: "Love begins as allurement—as attraction . . . The basic dynamism of the Universe is the attraction each galaxy has for every other galaxy."[1] Swimme describes the birth of a star as an example of what he is getting at:

> Imagine a vast dark cloud of hydrogen atoms stretching through millions of miles of space. Each of these trillions upon trillions of atoms is involved in an attracting activity for all the rest, and slowly begins to move. A common center emerges, and the hydrogen atoms begin to clump together. The growing pressure from the gravitational attraction enables the hydrogen atoms to fuse into helium atoms, thus releasing their hidden energy in a vast profusion of light emanating in all directions: the core of the star ignites. All of this activity is the result of the cosmic allurement of gravitation.[2]

Even though physics can name the basic attracting dynamics of the Universe and the laws that operate within them, it cannot say why they existed in that form in the first place. Gravity, electromagnetic interaction, and chemical attraction are deeply mysterious forces: "This attracting activity is a fundamental mystery . . . We understand details concerning the consequences of this attraction. We do not understand the attraction

1. Ibid., 43.
2. Ibid., 50.

itself."[3] Swimme tells the story of an event that happened to him shortly after he received his PhD in physics. He was sitting contemplatively, dropping a stone continually to the ground, when he realized that despite his academic achievement in science, he still could not understand why the stone fell. He says, "Before—and after—any theory, there is the ultimate mystery of the falling rock and the revolving Earth. The mystery remains no matter how intelligently we theorize."[4]

LOVE AND GRAVITY

In order to enter the mystery of the fundamental attracting powers of the Cosmos, one must first reflect on the fact that our Universe could have been different, operating on other laws that would have shaped it completely differently. However, this Universe, based on attraction and allurement, held together by gravity, is the one that we have to live in. Without this force, the Universe would disintegrate; in fact, it would never have formed in the first place. This attraction permeates all of reality. Swimme believes that it is the most primitive form and expression of love, a love that unites and thereby creates all that will follow, all that will flow out of the heart of love in an evolutionary stream: "Now you can understand what love means, love is a word that points to this alluring activity in the Cosmos. This primal dynamism awakens the communities of atoms, galaxies, stars, families, nations, persons, ecosystems, oceans, and stellar systems. Love ignites being."[5] We are accustomed to using the word *love* in an anthropocentric way—as human love—and have difficulty applying it to rocks and antelopes. However, Swimme would have us recognize that it is the basic energy of the Universe from which human love would eventually emerge. This is not sentimental. Consider the vision of Teilhard, which is the source of Swimme's inspiration:

> We are accustomed to consider . . . only the sentimental face of love . . . Considered in its full biological reality, love—that is to say, the affinity of being with being—is not peculiar to man. It is a general property of all life and as such it embraces, in its varieties and degrees, all the forms successively adopted by organized matter. In the mammals, so close to ourselves, it is easily recognized

3. Ibid., 44.

4. Ibid., 44.

5. Ibid., 49.

> . . . lower down on the tree of life, analogies are more obscure . . .
> If there was no real internal propensity to unite, even at a prodi-
> giously rudimentary level—indeed in the molecule itself—it would
> be physically impossible for love to appear higher up, with us, in
> 'hominized' form. By rights, to be certain of its presence in our-
> selves, we should assume its presence, at least in an inchoate form,
> in everything that is . . . Driven by the forces of love, the fragments
> of the world seek each other so that the world may come to being.
> This is no metaphor; and it is much more than poetry.[6]

Love, therefore, is not simply to be found in the human realm but
can be discovered in latent form throughout the Universe in all entities
since the beginning of time. It is the "principle of unification."[7] It propels
and lures creation to its destiny, that which Teilhard called the Omega
Point, where love will be all in all. He asserts that love is "the fundamental
impulse of Life . . . the one natural medium in which the rising course of
evolution can proceed."[8]

THE HOMINIZATION OF LOVE

It gradually becomes evident what Teilhard means by love evolving into
'hominized' form. Human consciousness is central to the evolution of the
Cosmos because it is here that love takes on human form, and Teilhard
believed that hominized love would be the medium that would allow the
Cosmos to reach its ultimate destiny—the transformation of matter into
spirit. We will look in more detail at this in book 3. Central to Teilhard's
vision is the rise of consciousness/love to such a heightened point (the
Omega Point) that the world dissolves or burns up with love. This con-
sciousness/love, which has been gradually unfolding in the Universe from
the beginning, takes on greater realization in the human being. There is
a clear hierarchy in Teilhard's thought that follows the rising path of consciousness through time. It is a hierarchy based on 'more evolved than'
rather than 'better than.' Human love is the most advanced form of love
that has developed so far; it is the Universe become consciously loving.
Teilhard's most famous statement arises from his vision of human beings,
through immense labor and the power of God, harnessing the supreme
force of love for God's purposes: "Someday, after we have mastered the

6. Teilhard de Chardin, *Phenomenon* of Man, 290–91.

7. Teilhard de Chardin, *Future of Mankind*, chap. 3, sec. 4.

8. Ibid., chap. 3, sec. 4.

winds, the waves, the tides and gravity, we shall harness the energies of love. And then for the second time in the history of the world, man will have discovered fire."[9]

ALLUREMENT AS GUIDE

Within human experience, allurement is experienced as a kind of gravity that pulls us toward a higher expression of love and a greater participation in life. Swimme believes that the strongest, deepest allurements we experience are the Universe's way of moving us in the right direction. Allurement does not refer to the superficial attractions that are continually pulling the human appetite in myriad directions—some of them very negative. When Swimme refers to allurement, he is speaking of a much deeper, more essential attraction that is experienced as an abiding tug to our hearts and comes from ultimate reality. Just as gravity moves the stars, so allurement draws the human heart to its own ends. Following these allurements ensures that we are doing our part in the ongoing journey of life—we make our contributions by following the directions within us. Joseph Campbell, the renowned mythologist, described this as "follow[ing] your bliss."[10] It is part of what Teilhard meant by "groping."[11] Along with all living entities, humans grope forward, drawn by their allurements, to explore every avenue that might lead to greater life. Allurements are the call of God within us and they can take many forms: art, music, beauty, passion, sex, affection, service, sacrifice. They draw us to moments of decision and choice, some minor and some profound, that will individually shape the course of our lives and communally shape the future of the Universe. When we follow our allurements we are responding to the invitation of ultimate reality to become all that we can be, and to build the kingdom of love. If we follow them, they will draw us into the heart of God.

Love, then, is basic to life in the Universe. It has been evolving and taking on higher forms as the journey of life progressed. Human love is the most explicit form (that we know about) that the Universe has produced so far. Swimme says that human love is characterized by an emerging sense of deep compassion, which is only in its infancy within

9. Teilhard de Chardin, "Evolution of Chastity," 86–87.

10. Campbell, *Power of Myth*, 120.

11. Teilhard de Chardin, *Phenomenon of Man*, 21.

human consciousness. It has the potential to become Godlike. During an interview, Brian Swimme said, "We are the first species that actually has the possibility of caring about all of the other species . . . suddenly you have the possibility, largely through the human imagination, of actually caring. My point is that the human being is that space in which the comprehensive compassion that pervades the Universe from the very beginning now begins to surface within consciousness. That's the only difference. We didn't invent compassion, but it's flowing through us—or it could. The phase change that we're in seems, to me, to depend upon that comprehensive compassion unfurling in the human species."[12]

It is important to note that this compassion for all beings is still largely undeveloped in the human race. Change occurs at a very slow rate, and it is incredibly difficult to get a sense of the big picture—of how humans are gradually becoming more compassionate. Perhaps we can get a glimpse of this by comparing the way people used to treat each other with the way they do now. Certainly, there is still terrible cruelty occurring within human societies around the globe, yet it is no longer normal to hang a child for stealing bread as it would have been several generations ago. People are more shocked now by acts of barbarism, and on the whole one could make a case for a rise in compassion. In any event, we obviously have a lot more growing to do in this regard, and there is nothing automatic about this. Freedom offers us the choice to love or hate at every moment, in every circumstance. When we choose love, the Cosmos advances; when we choose hate, we drag the world back away from its destiny. This sounds like a frustrating game of tug-of-war with the Cosmos being pulled now one way, now the other. Yet, the macro direction of the Universe is toward increasing compassion. I believe it is anyway; I am confident that Love, the originating power of the Universe, will draw us upward until we are home and Love is all in all. Choice remains and no one will be dragged kicking and screaming into the kingdom of love. Perhaps not everyone will make it, but in the end Love will not be denied.

DEVELOPING A TRULY HUMAN BRAIN

Neurobiologist Gerald Huther, in his challenging book *The Compassionate Brain: How Empathy Creates Intelligence*, contributes another perspective on this issue—one that shows us how far we have yet to go. He proposes

12. Bridle, "Divinization of Cosmos."

that the human brain is not being used to the fullness of its potential and has the tendency to get stuck in the rut of neural pathways that come easiest to it. In other words, humans tend to choose the path of least resistance and most comfort in dealing with the outer world of reality and the inner world of their thoughts, feelings and physicality. Not using our brains properly by challenging them with new ideas and self-questioning, and above all allowing them to feel "deep personal concern"[13] has led to a devastating shallowness and ego-centricity; devastating in its effect on the human and the whole human habitat. These are the actions of people who are operating with a deadened brain:

> They foul the air; alter the climate; pollute rivers, lakes, and seas; destroy the natural habitat; and squander the Earth's resources. They stand by and watch as more and more people lose the basic underpinnings of existence, as the rich variety of natural life forms and human cultures dwindles, as rain-forests are cut down, oceans are fished out, and fertile lands are turned into desert. They see all this plainly. Newspapers and television parade it before their eyes on a daily basis. But somehow they do not really feel a sense of deep personal concern about it. And as long as all these people manage to ward off and suppress the feeling of deep personal concern, they can and will go on behaving as they have, using their brains in the same old way.[14]

Huther tell us that we are still in the process of becoming fully human, to having fully functioning human brains, and we need to follow the path that will lead toward greater humanity. He says that we have two routes to choose from: the comfortable one of least resistance where we adopt the cultural norm and let it lead us by the nose into the deep rut of familiarity, or the uncomfortable one that faces the supremely human challenge of continual learning, that forces us to look around and within critically, and to change what is inhuman. For many of us, it takes a crisis to make us follow the second path. Most people "operating with ego-centered, shortsighted, one-sided, superficial, and thoughtless strategies, have to experience failure of breakdown on some level before they can get a look at themselves and understand the mistakes they have been making."[15] Huther believes that owning up to our mistakes is the first step

13. Huther, *Compassionate Brain*, 134.

14. Ibid., 135.

15. Ibid., 134.

in the right direction. If we cannot do this, our brains become robot-like and lose their chance to learn. A person who cannot change "has lost precisely that which characterizes a brain as human—the ability to step out of well worn ruts, to undo already existing programming."[16] Losing a sense of deep personal concern about the errors committed by individuals and societies is, according to Huther, the only really big mistake that we can make. He urges us to climb the ladders of "perception, feeling, knowledge, and consciousness."[17] Our decisions and subsequent behavior actually form the kind of brain we end up with: "The type and intensity of brain use determines how many connections are built up among the billions of nerve cells in it, what patterns of neuronal connectivity become stabilized there, and in how complex a fashion these neuronal connective patterns inter-connect with each other."[18]

How can we use our brains in a more comprehensive, complex fashion? How can the human race develop a truly human brain? Huther tells us that we must continually question what is most important in life. We must cultivate concepts such as "sensibleness, uprightness, humility, prudence, truthfulness, reliability, [and] courtesy."[19] We must seek out a community of like-minded people to help us. Most of all we must learn to love:

> Love creates a feeling of connectedness and solidarity that transcends the person loved. It is a feeling that keeps spreading outward until in the end it includes everything that brought us—and all the people we love—into the world and holds us here. A person who loves in this expansive way, without reserve, feels connected with all things, and everything that is around him is important to him. He loves life and takes pleasure in the multiplicity and colorfulness of this world. He enjoys the beauty of a meadow glistening with morning dew as well as a poem that describes it or a song that sings it. He feels a deep awe before everything that lives and that life brings forth, and he is sorely moved when any part of this is destroyed. He is curious about what there is to discover in this world, but it would never occur to him to take it apart out of pure greed for knowledge. He is grateful for what nature has given him. He can accept it, but he does not wish to possess it. All he needs are

16. Ibid., 135.
17. Ibid., 122.
18. Ibid., 123.
19. Ibid., 128.

other people with whom he can share his perceptions, his feelings, his experiences, and his knowledge. A person who wishes to use his brain in the most comprehensive manner must learn to love.[20]

Huther's book adds more weight to the argument that the development of compassion is the highest goal of human development. Reading his excruciatingly accurate depiction of the denial and suppression that continue in a society that is afraid to acknowledge its mistakes, makes humanity, at least in the West, seem irredeemable. However, his writings are not without hope. He acknowledges that the human brain is still a work in progress. Somehow, despite the terrible struggles with selfishness and hatred that plague human behavior, it is possible to see that we are still growing, still on the way, still young in love. Our ego obsessions as well as our addictions to violence and unhealthy practices may be more to do with our immaturity as a species than any intrinsic evil. We are only a very recent addition to the Earth community and not fully grown yet. Love, which is presently expressed immaturely, may yet flower within human consciousness in a way that would radically change the nature of life on Earth. Teilhard thought so, and so does Swimme. They believe that the energy of love, which empowers the Universe, is gathering strength within human beings—not because we are especially worthy vessels—but because Love itself is unstoppable. We are being carried along in a forceful current that is irresistible in its insistence on evolution. Somehow, humans will develop comprehensive compassion until a new way of living on the Earth has been born. Only in this way can the health of the planet be restored because compassion and empathy are the beginning of all fruitful change.

20. Ibid., 128–29.

4

Interrelatedness Within the Universe

ONE OF THE PRIMARY insights of modern science and the new cosmology is the interrelatedness of all reality, which makes up one organic whole, one outpouring, one energy event. In the modern world, when we want to understand something, we usually approach it by means of analysis, or taking it apart to study each thing separately. This can be helpful, but it is also problematic because it gives a misrepresentation of the true nature of reality. The sum of the parts does not make the whole. Now, we are moving beyond this to focus on the whole and the relationship between the parts. We are arriving at the recognition that nothing stands in isolation but is continually being acted upon and changed through interaction with that which surrounds it. Our guide, Brian Swimme, gives insight into this from the perspective of quantum mechanics:

> When electrons and protons interact with each other, protons are fundamentally and intrinsically changed. We say that the state vector is new, which means that we have a different reality than before. Why? The proton picks up something from its interaction with the electron. This is called quantum stickiness, and is central to the entire theory of quantum mechanics . . . That is how we study the reality of a thing, through its interactions and relationships. If these relationships are new, we have a new entity. An electron passing through hot plasma enters into different relationships; an atom in a highly charged electric field enters into new relationships; so does water passing down a mountain . . . Learning by analysis has been emphasized over the last two centuries, but we also learn by examining things as wholes.[1]

1. Swimme, *Universe is Green Dragon*, 88–89.

CONNECTIONS WITH THE PAST

We have already seen that there are no clear dividing lines between the different aspects of existence; matter, spirit, mind, consciousness, soul are all fluid terms which characterize one whole reality. Everything visible and invisible is permeated with the same basic stuff of the Universe in different forms. The human species does not stand in isolation as, historically, we have become accustomed to imagining ourselves; instead we are an integral part of the web of life on Earth and literally children of the Universe. As Brian Swimme often points out, we have to get over our horror of being related to everything. It is unfortunate that some people attribute human dignity to the fact that we are different from the rest of creation. I was watching a television program last week about intelligent design, which is another form of creationism. At one point, an evangelical Christian was interviewed regarding his feelings about evolution. There was real poignancy in his sadness about a perspective that could place monkeys and protozoa as human ancestors. He felt that this entirely demeaned human beings who, in his view, were the only creatures with souls, the only ones made in the likeness of God. I found myself wishing that he could view the entire Universe as flowing from the Godhead and rejoice in being kin to the stars, the ants, zebras and redwoods—each manifesting divinity within their own uniqueness.

Connected within the curvature of space-time, all that exists now in the present is a further development, a different expression of the primeval stuff of the fireball. Therefore, we can say we are made out of the stars and all matter is bio-spiritual in latent form. Self-reflexive consciousness did not suddenly appear with the arrival of human beings to the planet, but existed in embryonic form from the beginning of time. It was born out of the multiple levels and stages of previous consciousness. Swimme tells us, "If the fireball doesn't have a psychic dimension then I don't have a psychic dimension."[2]

It becomes possible to think of the Universe as 'remembering' the past in order to continue the creative enterprise of building the future. In a cosmic sense, memory is not just a faculty of human beings, but also a dynamic of the Universe. Memory is an activity: "Re-membering is something the Universe does. For the Cosmos, memory is the way the

---

2. Swimme, *Canticle to Cosmos*, 3.

past wakes in the present."[3] Matter does the remembering. Our bodies are "memory poured into flesh and bone."[4] Our genetic moldings evolved over millions of years, and our bodies remember their existence as stars. Swimme tells us, "The sequence of molecules that wake up your DNA is a sequence of memories."[5] The Universe remembers so that life can evolve in ever-greater sophistication, building on past developments, never forgetting any detail, never repeating itself, always probing and creating new possibilities. It is awe-inspiring to contemplate that nothing is lost; all is grist for further growth. Even the dead ends of evolution play their part because they are a necessary function of evolution. Life must grope forward and 'mistakes' are inevitable. All the extinct species of the past have played their part in the ongoing adventure of life.

A UNIVERSE OF HOLONS

We are indebted to innovative thinker Arthur Koestler for the term *holon*, which provides a way of understanding how nature is made up of the interconnection of wholes and parts. A holon is a whole that is also a part. While each entity is a whole in itself, it is always a part of something else. There are no wholes that are not also parts. For instance, as Ken Wilber explains, "a whole atom is part of a whole molecule, and the whole molecule is part of a whole cell, and the whole cell is part of a whole organism, and so on."[6] This is true not only for things but for ideas as well. There is nothing in the Cosmos that is not a holon. Even the entire Universe is not an autonomous whole because it operates within time; the Universe at this moment is a part of the Universe at the next moment.[7] Holons have two tendencies: to maintain their wholeness, and to fit in with their environment. They need to do both of these things simultaneously in order to survive. As I am writing this, I have to maintain the integrity of each idea, while at the same time I must see how each idea fits with the one previous and the one coming up next. If I did not do this, the writing process would be a jumble of nonsense. According to Wilber, holons also move into ei-

---

3. Swimme, *Universe is Green Dragon*, 102.

4. Ibid., 101.

5. Ibid., 101.

6. Wilber, *Brief History*, 20.

7. Ibid., 20.

ther self-transcendence or self-dissolution.[8] If a holon cannot maintain either its wholeness or its ability to fit in, it dissolves, but if it manages to do so, it climbs up to a higher level. A holarchy is a hierarchical system whereby holons move to higher and deeper levels. The direction of the evolution of holons is toward greater wholeness and greater communion. This sounds an awful lot like Teilhard de Chardin. Wilber tells us, "The drive to self-transcendence is thus built into the very fabric of the Kosmos [sic] itself."[9] As the holons move upwards they do not lose anything that has been gained so far because they include the lower level as they transcend it. The lower level is not destroyed but surpassed. As Teilhard predicted, matter is eventually transformed into spirit, which transcends and includes all else. Wilber puts this in his unique way: "Spirit transcends all, so it includes all. It is utterly beyond this world, but utterly embraces every single holon in this world. It permeates all of manifestation but is not merely manifestation. It is ever-present at every level or dimension, but is not merely a particular level or dimension. Transcends all, includes all, as the groundless Ground or Emptiness of all manifestation."[10]

Because the Cosmos is made up entirely of holons, no human or non-human subject can ever be truly independent. Interdependence is the way reality functions. The notion that human beings are in any way above nature is false. We are entirely related to everything within the web of existence. As Diarmuid O'Murchu points out in his book *Quantum Theology*, Western industrialism was flawed from its inception by its view, taken from the Newtonian physics of the day, that reality consists of "autonomous, isolated, independent objects."[11] It is no wonder then that the environment has been trashed by the Western mindset. Healing and renewal can only come from the realization, now emerging powerfully, that reality functions as a whole.

The activity of holons is captured visually by a machine called a hologram. A hologram is a kind of photography using a laser beam to capture a multidimensional picture of a subject. The subject emits a wave field of light, which becomes recorded on a plate as a pattern. A three-dimensional image is produced that has startling properties. Any section of

8. Ibid., 22.

9. Ibid., 23.

10. Ibid., 38.

11. O'Murchu, *Quantum Theology*, 53.

this image contains the whole picture within it. For instance, if the subject is a child and the part cut out of the image is the hand, then enlargements of the hand do not reveal a large hand but the whole of the child. The whole image is contained in any of its parts.

NON-LOCALITY AND PRAYER

If most of us were asked how we imagine the Universe, we would probably describe a lot of emptiness with some matter within it held discreetly in place by the force of gravity. In his essay "The Spirituality of the Earth," Thomas Berry insists on a new vision of the Cosmos: "The Universe is not a vast smudge of matter, some jelly-like substance extended indefinitely in space. Nor is the Universe a collection of unrelated particles. The Universe is, rather, a vast multiplicity of individual realities with both qualitative and quantitative differences all in spiritual-physical communion with each other."[12]

Every particle is connected together in this unbroken web of existence. Quantum physics describes a universal property called 'non-locality,' which is the activity of a particle in unmediated, sympathetic movement with another related particle. Even if vast amounts of space separate these two particles, if one is influenced, they both react in similar ways to the stimulus. Timothy Ferris aptly states, "It is as if the quantum world had never heard of space—as if, in some strange way, it thinks of itself as still being in one place at one time."[13] This means that the traditional law of cause and effect, which assumes that change is caused by local physical contact, is not the entire story. The Universe seems to act as a whole, which is much greater than the sum of its parts.

British biologist Rupert Sheldrake has been doing some very exciting work in the field of 'mental fields.' His findings are not accepted by mainstream science, but they offer provocative and intriguing insights into interconnectedness within the web of existence. He proposes that non-local causality occurs within fields of influence; that is, he believes that living beings are connected to each other over time and space within mental fields, and that they can influence each other through the power of thought and intention. The idea is that the mind is not situated only inside the brain or skull of an individual, but that it operates within a

12. Berry, "Spirituality of Earth," para. 9.
13. Ferris, *Whole Shebang*, 269.

field that can extend around the Earth. This is similar to the idea that Irish writer John O'Donohue speaks of in his book *Anam Cara*, where he describes the body as residing in the soul, not the soul in the body.[14] This counterintuitive view shatters the limitations of the extension of being. I recently heard someone describe her own being as enormous and far-reaching—far greater than her body could contain. Sheldrake sees the significance of his theory with regards to prayer:

> As soon as we have the idea that the mind can be extended through these mental fields, and over large distances, we have a medium of connection through which the power of prayer could work. We are no longer dealing with a purely mechanical system in the brain, with absolutely no way of connecting the brain and the observed effect—for if that were the case the phenomenon of effective prayer would have to be dismissed as delusion or coincidence. With a mental field, however, we have a medium for a whole series of connections between us and the people, animals and places we know and care about—with the rest of the world, in fact. When we pray, those extended mental fields would be the context in which prayer could work non-locally.[15]

This sheds new light on the importance of contemplative prayer. My sister is a nun in a contemplative order—she is a Carmelite. She is now sixty-six years old, and she has lived in her monastery since she was seventeen. I am quite sure that she does not need Rupert Sheldrake or scientific proof of any kind to convince her of the effectiveness of contemplative prayer. Her whole life has been dedicated to the firm belief that prayer can change the world. Different family members, friends, and acquaintances have viewed her commitment in various ways, ranging from admiration to horror that she has wasted her life. The latter reaction is caused by the conviction that action that can be externally observed is what gives significance to the lives we lead. My sister, however, has always seen prayer as the most profound and effective activity possible. For as long as I can remember (she left home when I was seven), Mary has been telling us that she dwells at the heart of the world where she can do the most good. She sees contemplative prayer as the movement down into the individual and out into the oneness where all reality connects, a journey from the particular to the universal. Personally, I have always felt wrapped within

14. O'Donahue, *Anam Cara*, 98.

15. Sheldrake, "Prayer," para. 13.

her prayers for me. Not that she believes it is simply a power that resides within herself that accomplishes so much good, but it is her union with divine power that is so transformative.

Rupert Sheldrake's research is interesting in that it provides another way of understanding the way prayer functions. It invites all people of loving intent to spread their thoughts and intentions of care and concern out to the troubled Earth. Whether we believe in a personal God or not, we can all do our part in the creation of a peaceful, caring world society, not only through outward activism but also through sending our love and compassion out to the world.

ECOLOGY AND GAIA THEORY

Interrelatedness, of course, has profound and revolutionary implications within the whole field of ecology. Countless biologists and environmentalists have been working tirelessly to convince us that all things, including humans, exist within ecosystems where each entity is dependent on every other one for its very survival. The most radical and vision-changing ideologies suggest that the Universe has no objects in it that can be manipulated thoughtlessly, but only subjects whose integrity needs to be respected. Thomas Berry is famous for stating that the Universe is not a collection of objects but a communion of subjects. James Lovelock gave us a world-shaking vision of the interrelatedness of subjects in his Gaia theory.

Lovelock proposes that life on Earth is one single, self-regulating organism. He named it after the Greek mother goddess, Gaia. Acting as a whole, life regulates the conditions on Earth so that a suitable condition can be maintained that will foster the continuity and expansion of life. It is a system that functions on the basis of interrelatedness and cooperation. According to this theory, the Earth maintains its oxygen levels and temperature within a range that will encourage life. For instance, the average surface temperature of Earth has remained between ten and twenty degrees Celsius for over three billion years. During that time the Sun's heat has increased by more than 30 percent, so something seems to be regulating Earth's temperature in a similar fashion to homeostasis within the human body. Just as our bodies are kept at a constant temperature by our internal organisms, so all of the living ecosystems of Earth cooperate in order to provide the stability of conditions necessary for life to thrive:

> The Gaia hypothesis . . . supposed that the atmosphere, the oceans, the climate, and the crust of the Earth are regulated at a state comfortable for life because of the behavior of living organisms. Specifically, the Gaia hypothesis said that the temperature, oxidation state, acidity and certain aspects of the rocks and waters are at any time kept constant, and that this homeostasis is maintained by active feedback processes operated automatically and unconsciously in the biota. Solar energy sustains comfortable conditions for life. The conditions are only constant in the short term and evolve in synchrony with the changing needs of the biota as it evolves. Life and its environment are so closely coupled that evolution concerns Gaia, not the organisms or the environment taken separately.[16]

This theory was ridiculed initially by skeptical scientists, but is gradually becoming part of mainstream science and is known as Earth system science. It has been an integral part of the deep ecology movement in its insistence that we exist within a web of life, an organic whole, which must be respected in order for life to continue to flourish. A colleague of Lovelock, Lynn Margulis, who worked closely with him to develop the Gaia theory, has made a significant impact on the scientific community and the ecological world with her related work on symbiosis.

In her book *Symbiotic Planet: A New View of Evolution*, Margulis describes an alternate view of evolution to that offered by mainstream biology, which has adopted the neo-Darwinist concept of natural selection. She argues that novelty occurs in nature, new species evolve due to what she calls symbiogenesis. The book explores the connection between Serial Endosymbiosis Theory (SET) and Gaia Theory. The key ideas of SET are incorporation, cooperation, collaboration, and teamwork. These stand in sharp contrast to the concepts of rivalry and competition that characterize the natural selection world. The emphasis is not on the survival of the fittest, but on the cooperation necessary in order to produce lasting, strong organisms. Symbiosis simply means "the living together in physical contact of organisms of different species."[17] Symbiogenesis means that new species eventually become established by "long-term permanent symbiosis."[18]

---

16. Lovelock, *Ages of Gaia*, 19.

17. Margulis, *Symbiotic Planet*, 2.

18. Ibid., 6.

Margulis does not propose a non-violent, harmonious cohabitation of organisms; rather, in order for novelty to emerge, organisms must be invaded and a battle must commence before the life-giving truce is settled. Two organisms, which are separately functioning entities, combine due to an urgent need in one of them, and eventually a new organism is produced by the cooperation of the two. This happened originally in the bacterial world. The cells of the plants and animal bodies of our present world originated through the merging of different types of bacteria which set up residence together.[19] There is a definite purpose for symbiosis, as life gropes always toward higher levels and greater novelty. We are all part of the dance of life: "Living beings defy neat definition. They fight, they feed, they dance, they mate, they die. At the base of the creativity of all large familiar forms of life, symbiosis generates novelty. It brings together different life-forms, always for a reason. Often, hunger unites the predator with the prey or the mouth with the photosynthetic bacterium or algal victim. Symbiogenesis brings together unlike individuals to make large, more complex entities . . . Symbiosis is not a marginal or rare phenomenon. It is natural and common. We abide in a symbiotic world."[20]

Margulis describes Gaia theory as symbiogenesis seen from space. The interconnecting organisms cooperate within a large-scale universality that regulates the Earth's environment like a huge homeostatic web. Gaia is tough, not fragile. It has been maintaining itself for billions of years, and humans should not take the view that it no longer knows how to protect itself. Many deep ecologists, certainly Thomas Berry, are frustrated and incredulous when humans speak of taking care of the Earth. Berry is outraged by the notion that humans are the stewards or caretakers of the Earth and views it as a sign of the anthropocentrism and arrogance of Western society. He insists that the Earth is a living entity that knows best how to take care of itself, and that human beings would do best if they stopped to listen to her: "The time has come to lower our voices, to cease imposing our mechanistic patterns on the biological processes of the Earth, to resist the impulse to control, to command, to force, to oppress, and to begin quite humbly to follow the guidance of the larger community on which all life depends. Our fulfillment is not in our isolated human grandeur, but in our intimacy with the larger Earth community,

19. Ibid., 30.
20. Ibid., 9.

for this is also the larger dimension of our being. Our human destiny is integral with the destiny of the Earth."[21]

We cannot take care of the Earth—the Earth takes care of us. That is not to say that we are not inflicting horrible damage on the planet at the present time and need to do everything we can to minimize our negative impact on the web of life. The point is that we must do this so that there is a future for human beings, and the species they impact, on the face of the Earth. If we do not correct the suicidal path that we are on, perhaps the Earth will reluctantly let us go and move on without us, gradually restoring its network of life and probing for new creative expression.

21. Berry, *Dream of Earth*, xiv.

5

The Role of Humanity

Landscape is the firstborn of creation . . . It is the most ancient presence in the world, though it needs a human presence to acknowledge it . . . In the human face, the anonymity of the Universe becomes intimate. The dream of the winds and the oceans, the silence of the stars and the mountains, reached a mother-presence in the face. The hidden, secret warmth of creation comes to expression here. The face is the icon of creation. In the human mind, the Universe first becomes resonant with itself. The face is the mirror of the mind. In the human person creation finds the intimacy it mutely craves. Within the mirror of the mind it becomes possible for diffuse and endless nature to behold itself.[1]

THE QUEST FOR MEANING and identity within the vagaries of existence has always spurred humans to ask fundamental questions: What does it mean to be human within the vastness of the Universe? Who are we, and what is our destiny? What is our role in the ongoing drama of planet Earth and the Cosmos? Philosophers have pondered the question of our identity for eons, but Brian Swimme gives us a fresh and provocative response that situates human life within the sweep of cosmic time. He states, "We are the latest, the most recent, the youngest extravagance of this stupendously creative Earth."[2] Human life has only existed for two million years, a fraction of the Earth's history. In Earth years, we are mere infants, still feeling our way into a mature relationship with the other life-forms and entities which comprise the Earth community. Most of our troubles arise not from evil intent, but from limited vision and extreme youth. Whether our species can survive until we grow up is another question.

1. O'Donahue, *Anam Cara,* 37–38.
2. Swimme, *Universe is Green Dragon,* 31.

HUMANS ARE THE SELF-AWARENESS OF THE UNIVERSE

We are children of the Earth; it gave birth to us after a labor of several billion years. We are the latest expression of the Earth's probing creativity, which in turn was born from the churning of the stars. Did we show up accidentally through chance, or was the Universe aiming for our emergence? This is a hotly debated question that scientists are divided on. Some would say that evolution is random in what it produces, while others discern principles of intentionality. In the latter camp, the anthropic principle proposes that the evolution of life is not only shaped by blind chance and necessity, but also by a self-organizing intelligence that seeks out ever more complex forms of expression and that seems to be oriented toward not only life, but toward self-reflexive consciousness. The new cosmology is in agreement with this principle: "At the heart of the Universe is a desire for life to unfold."[3] Physicists point to the constants in physics that seem to be arbitrary and unrelated and yet hold in common their orientation toward producing life and eventually consciousness. The Universe as a whole has certain properties that have allowed life and sentience to develop. The rate of expansion is not too fast and not too slow, the properties of matter are suited to life. They seem to be fine-tuned to produce the conditions necessary for these to evolve. For instance, gravity and electromagnetism are balanced in such a way as to allow stars to form. The nuclear weak force is precisely strong enough to allow hydrogen, and therefore water, to exist, while the nuclear strong force would have prevented protons, and therefore atoms, from existing if it had been a minute percentage stronger. A theory known affectionately as The Three Bears points to the fact that the Earth is not too hot and not too cold, not too big and not too small—in fact it is just right to produce life.

Swimme does not say that the Universe was aiming necessarily at human beings exactly as they exist today. Humans have evolved to the particular form that they manifest today because of the millions of adaptations and changes that chance and necessity have worked within life forms over eons. What he does say is that the Universe was destined to evolve into self-awareness in some form. Homo sapiens is just the one that came forth. Self-reflexive consciousness would have emerged at some point due to the inexorable probing of life towards higher forms. Humans are the highest expression of cosmic consciousness so far. In this

3. Swimme, *Canticle to Cosmos*, 2.

way, Swimme is in basic agreement with the anthropic principle. He says, "The closer we get to an understanding of the dynamism of the integral Earth, the more obvious it becomes that the four and a half billion years of terrestrial evolution resembles one vast embryogenesis. Something is developing, hatching, unfolding, and we are the self-reflexive mind and heart of the whole numinous process."[4]

On the one hand, humans need to be more humble about their place among the numerous species that manifest extraordinary intelligence and perception—much of it beyond our comprehension. On the other hand, nature has placed humans front and center on the Earth at this moment in time, and the kind of future the planet will have depends on us for now. Humankind has become so dominant that most of the other species and entities of the Earth are forced to exist within an anthropocentric framework. Human beings need to play out their essential role in the Earth's development by offering the fullness of their powers for the good of the overarching web of relatedness that forms the nature of existence.

Through humans, the Universe has developed a self-reflexive consciousness, an awareness of its own beauty, a heart, and a mind. This sounds shocking and almost ridiculous to our Western sensitivities trained in hard-nosed logic. Surely the words *heart* and *mind* can only refer to humans, not to the inanimate Cosmos? This statement only makes sense within the mindset we have been exploring. Our hearts and minds belong to the Universe, not only to us. We are the stars become able to think and feel: "We are the self-reflection of the Universe. We allow the Universe to know and feel itself."[5]

There is both a gift dimension and a risk involved in the evolution of consciousness. Until humans emerged, choice was limited by the determined genetic codings of Earth's creatures. The fixed action patterns of animals such as monkeys and whales are fuelled by instinct. These restrict their ability to shape their environment and behave creatively. With the emergence of self-awareness comes the possibility of freedom and choice. The book of Genesis, along with many other mythic stories, chronicles the possibilities for disaster that arrive along with these fundamental human attributes. Looking at the state of the Earth, it is clear that humans have not yet developed the wisdom and maturity to exercise their freedom in

4. Swimme, *Universe is Green Dragon*, 133.
5. Ibid., 58.

a responsible way. Self-awareness may be the destiny of the Earth, yet it has made itself terribly vulnerable in releasing such a dangerous force into the Universe. It is the vulnerability of the lover. Swimme wonders if the Earth will survive its love affair with human consciousness: "Earth in a sense wounded itself by allowing self-reflection to emerge. The human is dangerous precisely because the Universe is sublime. Here is the real question: Can the Cosmos survive the vision of its own beauty? . . . Can the Earth continue to organize its unfolding once its depths of eros have been tasted, their sweetness enjoyed."[6]

HUMAN GIFTEDNESS AND RESPONSIBILITY

So, who are we human beings who have arrived on the center stage of the unfolding drama of evolution? What gifts do we have to offer the ceaselessly hungry creativity of the Universe? Our gifts are many: our inventiveness; our cleverness with numbers; our capacity to dream and envision the future; our ability to use language and symbols; our capacity for relationship and sacrificial love; our humor and playfulness; our ability to create and appreciate beauty; the complexity of our abstract thinking. All these are great attributes, but they have a shadow side. Our giftedness can enhance the evolution of life on Earth, or it can hinder it. As many saints and mystics (not to mention movies such as *Star Wars*) have pointed out, humans have a tremendous capacity for good that can be perverted to evil due to the radical freedom we are born into. Christian theology catalogues seven deadly sins (lust, gluttony, greed, sloth, wrath, envy, and pride) that comprise a comprehensive list of normal human features that have become disordered through wrong choices. The wake of devastation that these sins leave behind in the human and non-human world could be endlessly catalogued. It is not difficult to see their natural healthy counterparts: sexuality, appetite for nourishment, ownership of necessary possessions, human labor, healthy anger, the desire for actualization, and self-appreciation. How vital it is that we learn to control and discipline the drives of human nature so that we can be a gift to the Universe and not a curse. Human powers need to be disciplined and focused wisely. When they are put to the service of the ego, they become monstrous. It is only a partial truth to say that humans have caused such harm to the planet because they are simply unwise and immature in the use of

6. Ibid., 75.

their powers. It is equally true to say that they have caused apocalyptic devastation to both the human and non-human community as a result of their sinfulness. Here, I mean sin as using human giftedness to satisfy the unchecked urges of the ego for power, wealth, status, possessions, and pleasure. Christian theologian Henri Nouwen spoke about living life with open hands.[7] By this he meant not grasping the gifts of life and holding onto them with a closed fist, but allowing them to be shared, to come and go freely from open hands. The challenge for the human race is to unclench our hands and release our giftedness for the service of life.

Perhaps one of the primary qualities of humans is our capacity for wonder. Brian Swimme believes that we are born to 'gawk'—to become entranced by the Universe through our careful attention and listening: "We awaken in the Universe bedazzled. We are the species of stupefaction."[8] He notices that the capacity to gaze and contemplate the beauty of the Universe is a particularly human quality. This very essential component of human nature has been deadened by urbanization and modern industrial life and needs to be awakened. We are closed off from the springs of creativity and ecstasy not simply by our lack of proximity to nature, but more by our reductionist, materialistic mindset. Thomas Berry submits that the characteristic, identifying attributes of humans have atrophied, leaving them in an isolated position within the Earth community: "We find ourselves in an autistic situation. Emotionally, we cannot get out of our confinement, nor can we let the outer world flow into our own beings. We cannot hear the voices or speak in response."[9] We are like autistic children, unable to freely communicate with the rest of the Earth community. How can we get back to the position our primal ancestors were in with regards to their intimacy with the Earth? It is not possible or fruitful to simply go back in time and lose all that evolution has given us. Swimme says that we do not need to return to the forest to live, we need to awaken to the miracle that life is. When we feel the Sun on our faces, we need to thrill with the awareness of the wild and extravagant energy that gives us life. Awareness brings gratitude and a desire to cherish the world in which we find ourselves an integral part. We need to be filled with awareness and amazement at the sheer miraculous and gorgeous nature of existence,

7. Nouwen, *With Open Hands.*
8. Swimme, *Canticle to Cosmos,* 7.
9. Berry, *Dream of Earth,* 17.

so that we will find the way to live in harmony with it rather than being a blot on it. How can we be "the space in which the Universe feels its stupendous beauty," if we do not live out our vocation to gaze and contemplate and become fellow artists of the masterpiece we find ourselves within.[10] The first step to healing is awareness.

Closely connected to our central capacity of gawking is our playfulness, our curiosity and desire to explore new possibilities. Biologists tell us that other mammals only spend a short period of their lives learning, playing, and being curious. This occurs when they are young and comes to a close as they leave adolescence and move into the more rigid period of adulthood. However, while other mammals experience these things only in the formative years of development, humans maintain, throughout their lives, a mature form of childhood. We are designed to keep playing and learning throughout our whole lives. We are unique in our capacity for humor. Swimme suggests "a deep belly laugh might be the one true cry of the human being."[11] Our curiosity leads to exploration, discovery, experimentation, inventiveness, and continual learning. Following what comes naturally in this regard seems to have got us into a terrible mess around the globe, but it has also produced truly fantastic inventions that have improved the quality of human life. Slowly, we seem to be learning through our painful mistakes that all people deserve a good quality of life, not to mention the natural world, and that the bounty which arises from our creative inventiveness needs to be poured out over the Earth, not hoarded for the satisfaction of a few. We have such a long way to go in this regard, but there is a groundswell at the grass roots level that seems to be stirring the sluggish conscience of the comfortable and causing the winds of change to blow.

REINVENTING THE HUMAN

Taking their cue from Teilhard de Chardin, Thomas Berry and Brian Swimme believe that the human race is poised on the brink of a new way of operating in the world, in fact, a new way of being human. As we have already seen, Teilhard proposed that there has been a gradual rise in consciousness within the Universe, which has culminated so far in the self-reflexive consciousness of human beings. He describes this movement as

10. Swimme, *Universe is Green Dragon*, 32.

11. Ibid., 122.

a gradual transformation of the world from matter into spirit. For him, human consciousness is not a static phenomenon, but it is on the rise to a higher form which will be characterized by convergence into unity or communion. This will eventually lead to complete union of the Cosmos with God beyond time. He calls this the Omega Point. Within Teilhard's vision, as human beings become more conscious and unified, they will become more sensitive and compassionate. They will be less ego-driven and locally oriented. This next step toward the maturation of the species, Thomas Berry has called reinventing the human.

Berry and Swimme make the radical suggestion that humans must reinvent themselves by reestablishing their communion with the Earth community and discovering their role within this context: "We will discover our larger role by reinventing the human as a dimension of the emergent Universe."[12] The human species is unique in its ability to continually invent itself. We are truly co-creators of ourselves. Berry says that we cannot achieve this by recourse to rationality because this is too limited by damaged cultural coding. By this he means that the cultures of the world have developed within a mindset that has gone astray, and they are, therefore, not equipped to move into the radical change necessary in order to reinvent the human. Rather, he suggests that story and dreaming are the paths to transformation: "The historical mission of our times is to reinvent the human—at the species level, with critical reflection, within the community of life-systems, in a time-developmental context, by means of story and shared dream experience."[13] By story, Berry means the telling of the story of the Universe, which has the power to awaken the human race into a realization of its origin and destiny within the Cosmos. By dreaming, he means awakening the deepest levels of human creativity that cannot be accessed through the rational mind but only through the human powers of imagination. He explains: "We are, of course, using this term not only as regards the psychic processes that take place when we are physically asleep, but also as a way of indicating an intuitive, non-rational process that occurs when we awaken to the numinous powers ever present in the phenomenal world about us, powers that possess us in our high creative moments. Poets and artists continually invoke these

12. Ibid., 18.
13. Berry, *Great Work*, 159.

spirit powers, which function less through words than through symbolic forms."[14]

Berry points to aboriginal peoples as well as poets and artists as leaders in this paradoxical process of awaking through dreaming. Through a renewed sense of the nature mysticism that has always characterized their "high religious tradition," they can teach the world reverence for the Earth, as well as the primordial spiritual unity of the cosmic, the human, and the divine.[15]

Thomas Berry's message to the world is one of hope not despair. His hope lies not so much in the ability of human beings to change things, but in the mysterious numinous power that is present everywhere in the Cosmos. He believes that humans are part of the great story of the Universe, and that they will be guided and given all that is necessary to carry out their role within the evolving world. He says, "We must believe that those powers that assign our role must in that same act bestow upon us the ability to fulfill this role. We must believe that we are cared for and guided by these same powers that bring us into being."[16]

Is it possible then, that humans, who seem to be in the middle of the greatest crisis of their era on the Earth, will soon develop the capacity to leave behind their destructive ways and re-vision their whole way of operating? Many of today's thinkers and commentators would suggest that the opposite is true—that we seem to be going backwards in our capacity to live in harmony with each other and our planet. Certainly, many of the more conservative followers of the various religious traditions believe that humans are moving further and further away from traditional values and moving toward hell in a handcart. They think that things are so bad now that an apocalyptic judgment day must be close at hand. How can Teilhard and his latter-day disciples be so hopeful?

To begin with, it must be clearly said that neither Teilhard, nor Berry and Swimme think that this breakthrough will simply come about as a matter of course. Teilhard is more optimistic than the other two, but they all agree that 'reinventing the human' will be a long, difficult process that can only come about if humans freely decide to co-operate in it. It is possible for humans to limit, tragically, their potential by failing to develop

---

14. Berry, *Dream of Earth*, 211.

15. Ibid., 184.

16. Berry, *Great Work*, 7.

their interiority and sensitivity to the world and choosing egocentrism over community.[17] Teilhard said that if human beings do not live up to their destiny, they will drag the world backwards into matter rather than allowing it to evolve into spirit. However, if they choose to develop their full potential, they will evolve to a higher state of consciousness, complexity, and unity.

What will be the cause of this seismic shift in human consciousness? Perhaps our mutual need for a way forward out of the terrible global crisis that is bearing down fast upon us will distract the nations from their warring and unite the peoples of the globe. Necessity has always been one of the greatest catalysts of change. However, Swimme and Berry think that the Earth itself will show us the way if we allow ourselves to move from arrogance and dominance into humility and attentiveness. The Earth can teach us if we are willing to be students. We cannot move into a new future until we awaken to the nature of reality by careful attention and listening. Swimme tell us that everything that has evolved in the Universe from the beginning has done so as a result of rapt attentiveness to the surrounding world and a desire to find its place within the epic journey. Our responsibility is "to develop our capacities to listen as incessantly as the hovering hydrogen atoms, as profoundly as our primal ancestors . . . The adventure of the Universe depends upon our capacity to listen."[18]

Most of all, the eros of the Universe will carry us forward if we are prepared to let it do so. In religious terms, the Spirit calls us to move upward. We need to recognize that the energy that draws us on is love itself. God wishes us to become love, the Universe itself is groaning in giving birth to Spirit.[19] A power greater than ourselves has seized us and carries us along. The allurement of the Universe draws us beyond the limiting and devastating lifestyle that presently exists. Swimme is quite clear that love is the force that gave birth to the Universe and that propels it forward. Our fullest destiny as humans is "to become love in human form."[20] Swimme says we need to fall in love, not just with the human race, but also with all expressions of the encompassing love within which everything exists, and indeed with love itself.

17. Teilhard de Chardin, *Phenomenon of Man*, 289.
18. Berry and Swimme, *Universe Story*, 44.
19. Rom. 8:9–22 (New Revised Standard Version).
20. Swimme, *Universe is Green Dragon*, 40.

6

Ever-deepening Differentiation, Subjectivity, and Communion

W HAT DOES IT MEAN to become love? This has been the abiding question of my life. The answer is simple and it is complex, involving both interior and exterior journeys into God. Thomas Berry and Brian Swimme present a trinity of concepts, which they call the basic laws of the Universe or the fundamental orientation of the Cosmos. This is one way of describing the movement into love: "The three basic laws of the Universe at all levels of reality are differentiation, subjectivity and communion. These laws identify the reality of the Universe, the values of the Universe, and the directions in which the Universe is proceeding."[1] This trinity of concepts did not come from empirical data but from what Berry and Swimme call a "post hoc evaluation of cosmic evolution." It arose from a close observation and contemplation of universal dynamics.[2]

THE REALITY OF THE UNIVERSE

To start with, it seems a good idea to name and describe what these three words mean. Differentiation refers to the unending diversity of all that exists. Each emerging entity, while maintaining similarities to all others, is unique and unrepeatable. Other words for differentiation are "diversity, complexity, variation, disparity, multiform nature, heterogeneity, articulation."[3] The movement of the Universe is into differentiation in time.

The law of subjectivity is about the inside nature or interior dimension of things. Other words given for subjectivity are "autopoiesis, self-manifestation, sentience, self-organization, dynamic centers of ex-

1. Swimme, *Canticle to Cosmos*, 4.
2. Berry and Swimme, *Universe Story*, 72.
3. Ibid., 71.

perience, presence, identity, inner principles of being, voice, interiority."[4] Within this vision, all matter has interiority and presence even if it is not living. Each thing is self-organizing: "Autopoiesis refers to the power each thing has to participate directly in the Cosmos-creating endeavor. For instance, we have spoken of the autopoiesis of a star. The star organizes hydrogen and helium and produces elements and light. This ordering is the central activity of the star itself. That is, the star has a functioning self, a dynamic of organization centered within itself."[5]

Finally, communion refers to the relatedness of all that exists. Other words for communion are "interrelatedness, interdependence, kinship, mutuality, internal relatedness, reciprocity, complementarity, interconnectivity, affiliation."[6] It is not possible for any one thing to live in isolation because relationship is fundamental to existence, and nothing can be itself without everything else. At every level of reality, communion exists.

Swimme describes these three as "cosmic grammar" and "the fundamental ordering of the Universe."[7] They are the natural laws that hold each thing in existence. Each one is necessary for anything to exist, and the wellbeing of all aspects of reality depends on their being kept in balance. For instance, if differentiation was taken away, then the Universe would be completely bland and homogenized with no possibility of newness and adventure. If subjectivity was removed, then there would no sentience, no depth, and no sensitivity. If communion was removed, the Universe could never have formed in the first place as matter would have flown apart and formed nothing. The laws are interdependent and interrelated.

VALUES OF THE UNIVERSE

When considered as values these three laws form the basis of a spirituality, a way of life that flows in harmony with the Cosmos and contributes to its ongoing evolution. Differentiation speaks of the need of each being to fully express its uniqueness in order for the world to unfold in richness and beauty. To be myself, to follow the vocation that the Universe hands me, is my task in life: "We are each given a quantum of energy at birth and we have this task to accomplish: identify who we are. It is our primary

4. Ibid., 72.

5. Ibid., 75.

6. Ibid., 72.

7. Swimme, *Canticle to Cosmos*, 4.

responsibility."[8] Differentiation hints at the prodigious generosity and desire for novelty of the originating power. It is beyond our imaginations to grasp that each emerging creation is new and unrepeatable: "The Universe comes to us, each being and each moment announcing its thrilling news: I am fresh. To understand the Universe you must understand me."[9]

Developing differentiation is an important task for each individual. It involves a careful listening to the fine-tuned, unique qualities that make each person different from everybody else. I must deliberately and consciously nurture the seed that was planted at my inception so that I can become as fully actualized as possible. Ultimately, my differentiation is a gift back to the Universe. As Teilhard would put it, I can help move the Cosmos forward into spirit if I contribute whatever is in me to the evolving beauty, truth and goodness of reality.

Nurturing differentiation takes discipline—it is hard work. It is joyful work because when I labor to give birth to myself, I must necessarily detect and then follow the allurements, the deepest passions, of my being. I often contemplate the virtue of discipline, and I acknowledge that for myself, and no doubt for most people, the lack of this is a huge loss to my ability to differentiate. Most of the time, I am very aware of what I need to do to grow, but so often ennui and procrastination take over. It is so much easier to follow the path most traveled—the one of least resistance. Perhaps that is why life is long—we need lots of chances to actualize our potential. The more we are able to do this, the more we can encourage and enable those around us to pursue their own destinies. Much of this happens by example rather than preaching. When we work hard at our own becoming, it is evident and inspirational for any discerning person who comes into contact with us. However, a deliberate effort to promote differentiation also involves seeing and promoting the giftedness of our family members, friends, work associates, and fellow citizens so that their unique powers can flow freely into the Universe.

In human beings, the cosmological imperative of subjectivity means that we must awaken and deepen our sensitivity to all subjects in the Universe. Because each being has interiority and, in a certain sense, a self, there are no objects in the Universe, only subjects worthy of respect, each one with its own value. Swimme submits that we come into the world

8. Ibid., 4.

9. Berry and Swimme, *Universe Story*, 75.

'half-baked,' with tremendous depth and sensitivity in latent form that needs to nurtured and developed. We can resonate with the joy, beauty and suffering of the world, or we can shut down our subjectivity into cynicism, and shallowness of every kind. It is tragic that the potential for deep subjectivity is sometimes squandered by people wasting their quantum of energy on distractions and shallow entertainments that cannot satisfy.

Human subjectivity can only be developed by a careful listening to, and contemplation of, the inwardness of each thing as a subject. This develops a tremendous sensitivity that allows us to experience life in an ever-deepening way. It takes sustained effort over a lifetime to really learn to see. When this is accomplished, we do not live in illusion. We resonate with reality in the same way that a crystal resonates with a certain note of music.[10] We take our experience of other subjects into our own interiority and develop a proper response to the dynamic nature of the Cosmos and to the contours of existence. For example, what would it mean to truly experience a tree so that its own subjectivity became present to us? Perhaps it would mean spending years being with it, watching it grow from a tiny sapling, becoming intimate with its uniqueness, being drawn into its world. Swimme passionately believes that each thing has a sacred depth that speaks of the numinous mystery of ultimate reality. Everything speaks if we listen carefully enough.

Swimme urges humans to immerse themselves in the natural world so that they can be transformed by the myriad manifestations of the Universe that have existed for millions of years before our species emerged on the scene. We cannot grasp the wider reality of the Universe when we live in such a tiny, anthropocentric world. We need to be present to allow the Universe to teach us and transform us: "When you walk into a forest, learn to tremble with the magnitude of what you are about, and you will never walk out. There will no longer be that self that approached the forest, for you will be new, you will bear the presence of the forest within you . . . The natural, human, and divine worlds flow together into our feelings. You need no teacher. The Universe is your teacher."[11]

Deep subjectivity requires silence and withdrawal as much as active participation in the world. Only in silence and solitude can the human heart interiorize the experiences of living in the Universe in an attuned

---

10. Swimme, *Canticle to Cosmos*, 4.
11. Swimme, *Universe is Green Dragon*, 95.

way. The spiritual discipline of subjectivity demands an exquisite attention to life, which uses every human sense and faculty, and also a sinking into the depth of silence in order to interiorize these experiences and touch their sacred depths. It is perhaps obvious to name meditation or contemplation as one of the major ways we can deepen our subjectivity. An amazing paradox lies at the heart of this type of practice: the experience of emptiness leads to the penetration of fullness; shutting down the senses fine tunes them to a state of alertness; entering the realm of no-thought sharpens consciousness to resonate with the meaning and mystery of the Cosmos. A disciplined practice of meditation allows us to see, hear, taste, smell, and touch with more finesse, greater depth, and increased sensitivity. Our minds become more open to the nature of reality in its glory and incompleteness.

It takes courage to deepen subjectivity because it means feeling more fully the pain and suffering of the Universe. Developing compassion arises from the same movement as deepening subjectivity. Compassion involves suffering with all those along for the journey, not hiding from the dark side of life, but embracing our own pain and that of our fellow travelers in order that we may reach our destiny together. On the other hand, deepening our subjectivity gives us a taste of heaven, of the possibilities for joy and ecstasy that dwell at the heart of the world. It is part of the process of becoming love.

As a cosmological imperative, communion urges us to recognize that the Universe is comprised of a community of subjects. A recognition of this might lead to greater harmony within the Earth community instead of the wholesale destruction of the many species for the sake of the one. We need to recognize that when we harm the Earth, we harm ourselves—such is the web of life: "As we are tearing apart the rain forests, we are destroying our own body."[12] Ever-deepening communion is not just a nice ideal, it is a necessity—without it nothing survives. Swimme describes the loss of relatedness as "a kind of supreme evil in the Universe . . . To be locked up in a private world, to be cut off from intimacy with other beings, to be incapable of entering the joy of mutual presence—such conditions [are] the essence of damnation."[13]

12. Swimme, *Canticle to Cosmos*, 4.

13. Berry and Swimme, *Universe Story*, 78.

Choosing to enter into communion with the Universe means choosing to become love. In essence, love is the union of all beings, the Universe beating with one heart. Communion always involves reaching beyond our own needs and desires, pouring ourselves out for the good of the other. Therefore, an essential aspect of deepening communion is to be committed to social and Earth justice—striving for the betterment of all the people on the planet as well as all the other members of the Earth community. It means recognizing that my own happiness is a mirage unless it is rooted in the wellbeing of the whole. Communion involves receiving as well as giving; in fact ecstasy could be defined as giving all and receiving all. Surely, this is the secret of becoming love.

THE DIRECTION OF THE UNIVERSE

Finally, Berry and Swimme speak about these three in terms of the aim of the Universe or the direction in which it is going. Book Three explores eschatological matters and the possible direction the Universe is traveling in. The trinity we speak of here provides a sense of this future. Swimme says, "The ultimate aim of the Universe is a fullness of differentiation, the deepest of subjectivity, the most intimate communion."[14] These three fundamental laws or values of the Universe also provide the nature of its destiny and fulfillment. We do not live in an indifferent Universe, blown about by the winds of chaos; we live in a Universe that has had an aim since it first erupted out of the fireball. Its direction, fuelled by the love that formed the originating power of the Universe, is toward an intimate communion of fully differentiated beings, each one resonating with the deepest capacities of subjectivity and sensitivity.

Swimme does not speak about a supernatural future for the Universe. For him, nature itself contains the transcendent elements that religion traditionally associates with a heavenly realm. He believes that there is no outside to the Universe—that it is one, unified, material, spiritual mystery, and that heaven is one dimension of existence within the Universe. It is its fulfillment. What he tells us about differentiation, subjectivity, and communion can provide an inkling of what the ultimate aim of the Universe is, what the promise of existence is. In this kind of heaven, each created thing would have reached its ultimate potential in unique giftedness, each entity would be as fully itself as possible—there is no blending or homog-

---

14. Swimme, *Canticle to Cosmos*, 4.

Book II

Cosmic Suffering

So far, we have looked in a general way at the vision of reality made possible by the new cosmology. There are so many directions one could take in exploring a spirituality generated by this, and the ones I have chosen are simply those that speak most strongly to me within my own search for ultimate meaning. As well, I am loosely following the flow of the fundamental questions of life: Where did we come from? What does life mean? Where are we going? The topic of suffering fits within the second question. It confronts me in an immediate and compelling manner. I imagine that I am a very typical human being in this regard. The nature and purpose of suffering is the ancient and, in many ways, indecipherable conundrum that has baffled and shaken us throughout the ages. These chapters reflect my own musings as I look at the mystery of suffering within the insights of the new cosmology.

FINDING OUR BALANCE

I believe that good literature, like any true art, gets to the heart of human existence more exquisitely and precisely than any other discipline. Rohinton Mistry's novel *A Fine Balance* is a case in point. Although it is about many things, I think that this is, above all, a book about suffering and the choices it offers to human beings. *A Fine Balance* is set in Mumbai, India, between 1975 and 1977 when Prime Minister Indira Gandhi declared a state of emergency, causing acute tension that erupted into racial violence. It is about four characters: Dina Dalal, a widow trying to maintain her independence in a society where women are expected to be dependent on men; Ishvar Darji and his nephew Omprakash, who are untouchables trying to better themselves through becoming tailors; and Maneck Kohlah, a student from a middle-class family. Their lives intertwine, and they influence each other's destinies. Although all of them suffer due to "the slings and arrows of outrageous fortune," the locus of pain is centered in the two untouchables, who represent every downtrodden, vilified, dehumanized, discounted, marginalized, ostracized, shunned, despised, poor person who lives on the face of the Earth. Every imaginable horror happens to them until the reader can barely continue to follow their story. By the end of the book, Ishvar's legs have been amputated, and Omprakash has been castrated, ensuing in his body swelling up from the hormone changes.

Before you decide never to read this incredible book (which won Canada's Giller Prize for fiction), I must say how deeply moved I was by it. The character that I identified with most (and I imagine this would be true for the majority of readers in our comfortable, protected world) was Maneck, the student, who does not have to endure any unusual pain himself but is overcome in the end by the suffering of humanity (in particular that of his two friends) and kills himself violently by stepping in front of a train. The strange twist at the end of the book is that the two untouchables find a kind of peace and happiness, despite their unspeakably difficult lives. They are the ones who remain cheerful, finding a 'fine balance,' while the one who cannot endure the pain of the world dies in despair.

After I had read the last page of *A Fine Balance*, I closed the book and began to cry, long and hard, from the bottom of my soul. It was as if a well of unexpressed sorrow was pouring out of me. I was Maneck, unable to face the suffering of humanity. Like him, I struggled to find meaning in the brutish, foul mess that seemed to comprise much of human existence in the world. Although personally I experienced many joys and comforts, these did not sit well with me when I considered that so many of my brothers and sisters around the world were living in horrible pain.

The book touched a nerve in me that had always been tender. From an early age I decided that, overall, life was not a good thing. I came to the conclusion that the pain involved with living and dying weighed heavier in the balance than the joy of being alive. One of the vivid memories of my childhood is an episode of awakening to disillusionment. No doubt this experience was due, in part, to the anxiety and depression problems I suffered from in my childhood. I was simply lying on the sofa in the front room one day when I was about nine, feeling the strange disembodiment that anxiety brought with it, when I suddenly saw that most moments in life were not happy but contained a mixture of restlessness, regret, and worry. Even when life was going well, the human psyche seemed to be fretting and struggling over the business of being alive. And underneath it all, I detected a sense of meaninglessness about the continual round of mundane existence. Every experience of happiness was tinged with sadness—every moment of joy was not only fleeting, but also not enough. "Is this all there is?" I wondered. "How can we live with such incompleteness and misery?" I was well aware that I was one of the lucky people who lived in a loving family that could provide all the necessities of life. What haunted me was the thought of what life must be like for the countless people on the planet with few or none of those things. I could not imagine why anyone really wanted to live, and I began to see life as a difficult journey that would have to be navigated, somehow, so that I could die and go to heaven. I tried to plot the safest life possible that would get me through with the least amount of suffering. I began to fantasize about being like my eldest sister, living in a contemplative order, and being surrounded by loving companions who would take care of me.

Of course, my sister's life is nothing like the hiding place of my imagination, but at that point it looked like the safest kind of life to me, and I am sure this mindset contributed to my entering religious life myself in my mid-twenties.

Life took on the aspect of a disease that we were all inflicted with. I developed a sense of anger at my parents for giving birth to me and at God for forcing me against my will to live my life. Why didn't God ask my permission before giving me life? Where was my freedom of choice not to exist? In my imagination, non-existence was a wonderful fantasy—I would not be able to feel anything at all. I used to invent scenarios where somehow everyone on Earth would decide not to procreate any more, and that after a hundred years there would be no more human presence on the planet. How peaceful that would be.

Another traumatic time for me was during the sixties when it seemed only a matter of time before atom bombs would destroy the world. I was a teenager by then and resolved that I would never bring children into the world. I would never have a child of mine vulnerable and exposed to such a dangerous place. Despite my belief in a loving deity, I ranted and raved at God for creating life the way it was.

As I matured, I gradually found a degree of healing and peace, and this brought with it a tentative desire to trust in the goodness of life. In my mid-thirties, I decided to leave religious life where I had been hiding (it was a good deal more than that, but I gradually had to face the truth that I was hiding out), hoping to stay at the edges of life, and plunge into the deep end of experience by getting married. This break was terrifying for me in many ways, and at the time I experienced recurrent, violent nightmares where I was being murdered. However, the new hope that I felt overcame my fears, and I chose to live life as fully as I could. I married; I even trusted enough to have two children, although I confess there have been many times when I have been overcome by fear at their vulnerability in the face of suffering and danger. Sometimes, I have felt bitter and remorseful about bringing them into the world, although they have always proven to be much stronger than I imagined.

I am trying to describe to you the battle that has been going on inside me all my life between hope and despair, trust and mistrust, faith and utter doubt, meaning and meaninglessness. I would be surprised if you did not have similar stories to tell me. The human struggle to believe in the goodness of life is always faced with the sometimes insurmountable problem of suffering. Why is there suffering?—this question always has been and always will be at the center of the search for ultimate meaning. Personally, I have spent too much of my life vacillating between trusting in the goodness of life and despairing about the suffering in the world. I am not proud of this; I think that it is a form of cowardice. I credit the insights I have received from the new cosmology and my stubborn faith in a loving God in drawing me toward the positive side of the equation. I cannot say that I will always react well when I am faced with suffering, but I believe I am moving in the right direction. The following chapters contain the insights that have helped me on my way to find a fine balance.

7

Natural Causes of Suffering

ALL LIVING THINGS SUFFER. I believe St. Paul was quite correct to de-scribe the whole Universe as groaning on its birthing journey within the contours of space and time.[1] Human beings suffer in a particular way, and, in the end, it is the only type of suffering we can truly comprehend. We do not know what it is like to be an animal, let alone a plant or a rock; we only know what it is like to be human. However, in order to get to the natural roots of human suffering—that is the pain that is caused simply by being alive on planet Earth before human complexities muddy the waters with the consequences of freedom and choice—it might be helpful to remove human beings from the picture for a moment and simply look at the nature of the Cosmos. What is it about the natural order of the Universe that brings about suffering for sentient beings?

LIVING ON THE KNIFE-EDGE

It is obvious, as soon as one opens any book on cosmology, that the Universe journeys through time on the edge of a knife, miraculously es-caping total annihilation by a cat's whisker. Learned scientists inform us that the Big Bang produced equal amounts of particles and anti-particles, but the fact that matter took shape over the course of time and was not totally annihilated by anti-matter means that somehow a tiny imbalance must have developed which favored matter. This incredibly fine-tuned birthing process allowed the whole Cosmos, including you and me, to evolve. These early beginnings, occurring in unimaginable heat and den-sity, set the scene for a portentous, mind-shattering drama unparalleled in human literature. The forces of chaos and the armies of order clash in such cataclysmic violence that it is barely within the grasp of human

1. Rom. 8:18–23 (NRSV).

imagination to picture it. Terrible destruction and incredible beauty live side by side. Fine-tuned, exquisite elegance balances on the brink of abominable disorder. (I am sure you have noticed by now that it is impossible to keep human perceptions out of this!) Violence and beauty live as lovers intertwined and inseparable.

Right from the first fraction of a second of its birth, the Universe flared out of its cosmic egg in a riot of ruin and triumphant form, continually destroying and creating itself anew. From the beginning, destruction and violence were absolutely necessary for the emergence of variety and novelty. And so it continued. The early formations, the galactic clouds, had to be destroyed in order to produce stars, and cataclysmic supernova explosions were necessary for the emergence of new constellations and, eventually, the conditions necessary for life on planet Earth, a speck of a planet in a minor galaxy in an obscure corner of the Universe. If the star Tiamat had not been destroyed in a supernova explosion, then the Milky Way solar system would not have emerged, and neither would the Earth or life as we have come to know it. Berry and Swimme tell us that "[o]ur birth required the drastic and vehement disruption of well-ordered communities of being."[2] The Cosmos exists within the tremendous mystery that the opposing poles of destruction and creativity thrive together, causing continual change and novelty as the world evolves through time and space. This is the reality that orders existence.[3] Chaos theory informs us that the reason we witness the triumph of form is because, overall, order seems to emerge from randomness, or it may be more accurate to say that there are patterns of order inherent within chaotic systems. The essential point here is that the two are inseparable; they are major players in the great balancing act of the Universe. It is all so astonishing to contemplate. We take for granted the 'isness' of our world, but we live within impenetrable mystery. The fact that we are here at all is miraculous.

RESISTANCE, FULFILLMENT, AND ENTROPY

Let us take a closer look at some of the laws that govern this sensational drama. In their wonderful book *The Universe Story*, Swimme and Berry identify three ways in which the Cosmos regulates itself (all of which, from the human perspective, cause terrible violence and suffering): the

2. Berry and Swimme, *Universe Story*, 49.

3. Ibid., 51.

Pauli exclusion principle, the tendency of matter toward ultimate development, and the second law of thermodynamics.

The Pauli exclusion principle, formulated by Wolfgang Pauli in 1925, identifies the fact that all matter resists other matter. It states that no two particles can occupy the same quantum state, and that any entity will fiercely resist being overcome by any other entity. It is as if each individual particle is determined to exist and defend its turf against invaders. It claims its own exclusive space. If two particles meet, they do not simply pass through each other but collide, creating the potential for adversity and violence.[4] Although it is obviously one of the fundamental reasons why anything survives and flourishes, this principle of the self-protection of matter causes an arena of monumental struggle throughout the natural world. In human society it is expressed not only in the rights of the individual, but also in anarchy and warfare.

Secondly, everything that exists has an in-built tendency to move towards the fulfillment of its own potential. It is natural for all entities to strive for the achievement of as much development as possible.[5] A plant will lean toward the light to maximize its capacity to grow; a lion will prey on weaker animals in order to become strong; a swarm of locusts will not hesitate to devour a field of corn so that it can thrive. This tendency has produced magnificent life forms, but it rests upon competition for free energy and the law of the jungle. In human society it is expressed not only in stunning accomplishments and fulfilled dreams, but also in competitiveness, selfishness, and greed.

The second law of thermodynamics, sometimes called the law of increased entropy, is by itself the most devastating cause of suffering in the world. It states that within a closed system (such as the Universe) usable energy is continually converted to unusable energy and that eventually, over time, everything winds down and is lost. Entropy is sometimes called the arrow of time. As the world moves forward in time, entropy increases. There is an inherent tendency within the natural process toward loss of energy. The Universe had a beginning and possibly it will have an end when all useful energy has been dissipated (this is only one of the end-of-the-world theories). Everything within the Universe requires a steady supply of energy. The Sun, which provides such a massive outpouring

4. Ibid., 52.
5. Ibid., 53.

of energy onto the Earth, will one day use up all of its own energy and die. Creativity is incessantly at work bringing forth new developments, but this does not come cheap; there is an energy cost that must be paid for each new birth.[6] In human society this law is expressed not only in the birth of new people and emerging ideas, but also in death and decay. The march of time means that change and loss are simply givens. The passing of the old makes way for the arrival of the new, but this cycle is tremendously difficult for humans to deal with. Death is inevitable—our bodies and minds wear out. Each newborn baby begins to die with its first breath. Everything that is built up must crumble and decay.

Each of these natural forces brings strife and suffering, yet they also balance each other. They provide the creative tension necessary for life to proceed on its journey toward ever-increasing complexity, unity and beauty: "These obstacles, these boundaries, and these limitations are essential for the journey of the Universe itself."[7] Resistance causes the creation of mountain ranges; the drive for fulfillment causes symphonies to be written. The law of entropy protects the integrity of the whole by limiting the capacity of each part. The truth of the last statement can be demonstrated by a look at aphid populations. The aphid is such a tiny insect, yet it could upset the balance of life on Earth if it was able to follow the principles of self-preservation and expansion without the balance of entropy and energy cost. In a single year, aphids could generate enough offspring to destroy the Earth.[8] The balance of demand and constraint, or need and limitation, is what shapes the Universe. Everything is about balance and equilibrium. If the energy requirement is ignored or avoided, then the forces of self-preservation and development become monstrous. Without the energy cost described by the second law of thermodynamics the world would lose its balance and topple into oblivion. Constraint and limitation initiate the necessary tension to hone and fine tune creativity.

Suffering is an absolutely necessary and indispensable part of life in the Cosmos. It is not intentionally inflicted, but it is the inevitable consequence of the way the Universe is shaped. Pain for the sake of pain is abominable; suffering for a purpose is more bearable. The contention of this book is that the purpose of suffering is to allow the Universe to evolve

6. Ibid., 52.

7. Ibid., 55.

8. Ibid., 54.

into more expansive, refined forms of beauty and love, and ultimately to find its way home to the heart of love. Subsequent chapters will explore this destiny. Within the natural context, it makes sense that the Cosmos can only maintain its existence and reach for further horizons if it continues within its present tensions and structures. Within a religious context, to ask why God allows suffering in the world is to ask why God allows the world to continue.

8

Human Responses to Pain

IT IS ALL VERY well to speak about the necessity of violence and destruction in the natural flow of things. It all seems so logical and understandable. But to place human beings into this context is to introduce a whole new set of elements that call into question the symmetry and logic of the whole system. In fact, human presence in the Universe can seem like a mistake, an alien invasion, a round shape in a square hole. The emergence of self-reflexive consciousness brings with it not only exquisite suffering caused by a heightened awareness of, and sensitivity to, the painful balancing act of the Cosmos, but also the nature-destroying mechanisms that humans have mastered in order to defend themselves against such a difficult existence. History has only lately started to tell the story of how human beings have upset the applecart of life on Earth with their determination to not fit in with the natural order of things. Berry and Swimme convey the vulnerability of the human experience, the sensitivity of the human race to the pain that naturally arises from the laws of the Universe: "Within self-reflexive consciousness, terror becomes aware of itself. With such conscious self-awareness, life understands that it is precious and liable to destruction."[1]

HUMAN VULNERABILITY

Humans are beset with many kinds of particular pain that are unique to our kind. Our consciousness allows us to be unsettled and anxious about change and the unknown future; we feel the agony of loss in its myriad forms; we can anticipate suffering, thus intensifying its impact; we have knowledge of our certain individual deaths and worry about the death of our loved ones, and indeed, our species; we feel depression and despair

1. Ibid., 56.

at the limitations which fence us in; our complex minds can become sick and overwhelmed by the demands of living; in moments of terrifying clarity, we understand that we are tiny, pinpoints of life in the vastness and the darkness of space. I'm afraid the list continues on; it is not easy being human. No wonder we make so many mistakes.

Sometimes, it seems that the human race is an anomaly on the face of the Earth, as if we got lost and ended up here by mistake. Human beings cannot seem to reconcile themselves with the way nature operates. Why are we continually surprised and shocked that life is not only pleasurable and delightful but also difficult and painful? Why haven't we long ago accepted that this is so? When we look around ourselves at the animal kingdom, we get the distinct impression (although necessarily an anthropocentric one) that our closest relatives on the tree of evolution do not fret about the contours of existence the way we do. It seems that this existential angst arises from the complexity of our self-reflexive consciousness. Did our early ancestors have a problem with the meaning of life, or did this uneasy questioning arrive with civilization? Given the evidence of ancient burial rites and the myths that are common to all early human communities, it seems that we have been trying from the beginning to make sense of the world and to extract a sense of meaning for our lives. The only way any life form can flourish or even continue to exist is to feed on other life forms. This cannibalistic mode of being has always deeply shocked the human psyche, and mythology reveals the ritual attempts of early peoples to harmonize their existence with this dark side of nature. Why do we humans have such a difficult time finding our balance in the world?

LEARNING TO TRUST

Theologian John Haught presents some interesting ideas from process philosophy that might give us a clue about why we do not cope very well with the nature of things. He suggests that a good part of our suffering comes from a lack of trust in the beneficence of nature, that if we were more in touch with a global, cosmic sense of the whole mystery, we would trust more and suffer less. Part of the reason that we feel such pain, and consequently behave so badly, is that we float on the surface of existence, busying ourselves with the mundane instead of taking the plunge into the depths of life where we would discover its heart and, therefore, its purpose. Our sensitivity to suffering may have a lot to do with our perception of reality.

If Alfred North Whitehead, the father of process philosophy, is correct, it appears that humans do not simply observe the world as it is moment to moment, we also perceive reality in a kind of global, diffuse way. Within this universal perception we are dimly aware of the wholeness or oneness of things. In our local perception we experience what is immediately around us through our senses. Haught simplifies Whitehead's language by calling the former our "primary perception" and the latter our "secondary perception."[2] Process thought is so called because it defines reality as process rather than product. At every moment, creation is rising and passing away, so that we are not really aware of the actual present, because it has already slipped into the past before we can grab it. What we call the present is actually the immediate past. Everything is always in process. We can remember the distant past as far as our memories allow us, but Whitehead proposes we can also perceive the accumulated experiences of not only our own personal past, but the past of the Universe as well. This goes along with the insights of modern science that everything is interconnected and organically tied together within time and space. We have seen from Book One that who we are today has evolved from the ancient, primordial past, and that somehow that past is still present to us, both in the tissues of our bodies and in the deepest recesses of our consciousness. Our own self-reflexive consciousness is an aspect of the Universe. Whitehead, therefore, concludes that the entire past of the Universe is also present in a diffuse way in our perception. He submits that, in being too materialistic, the scientific community has led society into a myopic way of perceiving reality—has narrowed down perception to only the secondary kind, that is sense perception, and that it has rejected the vague and immeasurable data that comes from primary perception. In order to function in the world with sharpness and clarity, secondary perception is vital. The mind necessarily refines and focuses awareness so that we can get on with the tasks of daily life, but that does not mean that primary perception can be ignored or rejected. Our sense perception only presents us with a surface layer of reality, and we are in danger of losing a truly cosmic perspective if we limit ourselves to only that.

2. Haught, *Cosmic Adventure*, chap. 12, para. 5.

One of the most acute causes of psychological and spiritual pain is our inability to trust the Universe. We are shocked and surprised at the functions of nature because we find the whole process of being-in-the-world untrustworthy. This is because, for the most part, humans spend too much time operating within secondary perception and not enough time rooting themselves within primary perception. It is only at the subliminal, unconscious level that humans can experience both oneness with all of reality and deep trust that all things have ultimate value and meaning. Haught tell us that "it is in primary perception that we feel the ultimate beauty and value that gives actuality to all that is. This primary organic contact with the Cosmos infuses us with a subliminal sense of the world's value, and we give evidence of this primordial awareness in our tendency to trust."[3]

Much of modern life in the West invites us to live almost entirely within the realm of secondary perception, which is the local world of our senses. The image of a small boat bobbing on the surface of a vast ocean captures the limitations of our secondary perception. We miss most of reality; the fine balance of existence is skewed. Western society is incredibly efficient and successful at operating at the explicit, outward, practical level of life, but hopelessly unbalanced in terms of its inner life, which is parched and shrunken. This lopsided way of operating has many negative repercussions, but perhaps the most devastating consequence of losing our connection to primary perception is our inability to trust in the world.

The primary perception can only be touched in practices such as meditation, contemplation, inwardness, deep reflection and through experiences of transcendence or ecstasy. We connect to the cosmic depths of life through the language of symbolism rather than the discourse of the rational mind. We can be taken from the limited, local experience of the mundane world into the knowledge of oneness and the perspective of the big picture where the yin-yang polarities of reality find their home within the whole. Religion is one (but not the only one) of the major gateways to primary perception. Trust may be in a personal God who has "the whole world in his hands," or in the world itself which is identified with divinity in a monistic oneness. The many paths of religion all take the seeker below the surface of secondary perception into the realm of deep primary

3. Ibid., chap. 12, para. 3.

perception and to the peace that trust brings. At this time in the West, when religion has been largely rejected by mainstream society, there is a deep hunger to find spiritual depth and connectedness, which has found expression in many contemporary movements. We live in a time of seeking new paths into the heart of life.

At this point, I feel the need to interrupt the flow of these inspiring ideas to give voice to my cringing, fearful self, which is agitated by the notion of putting its trust in the Universe. I want to protest that life (the world, God, the whole process of existence) is certainly not trustworthy. After all, we have just seen that the laws that govern the Cosmos are bound to result in suffering and death. How can we possibly trust something that is going to hurt us? Don't we usually trust someone or something because we believe we will be protected from harm?

The best answer that I can give myself comes from my Christian background. It is inspired by the image of Jesus on the cross. He trusted in God even though he was in the farthest reach of suffering in his body and his spirit. He trusted God, not because he thought he would be protected from suffering or because he knew that he would be raised from the dead, but because he knew that God was caring for him in a way that transcends both life and death. He knew that God is love and that within the embrace of that love, he would be safe even while he was being destroyed. At the level of secondary perception, his life ended in disaster; at the level of primary perception, his life reached its triumphant conclusion because he trusted in the goodness of God. Jesus lived and died heroically. Despite our cringing, fearful shrinking back from suffering, we are called to the same heroism. It is the only successful response to life.

Christian readers may be confused and even insulted by the way I am blending God and the Universe here. They may feel that God is absolutely trustworthy, but the world is absolutely not. I am sympathetic to those feelings. Until I came to embrace the belief that the Universe is the primary revelation of God, I thought of God and the world as two separate and even opposing realities. My trust was entirely in God who I believed would save me from the world. I thought of God as someone who would protect me from pain and disaster, intervening in the natural processes of nature and forming a safe haven from the terrors of existence. It seemed to me that God was for humans and that the rest of nature, even though it was created by God, was just background—sometimes lovely, sometimes threatening, but incidental to the important ideas of religion, like salvation and eternal life. Now, I understand the world as being part of God, as being within God, just as a baby is inside its mother's womb. Like all metaphors, this one is inadequate, yet it speaks to me more powerfully than any other I have come across. I feel enwrapped with care and loving-kindness—free-floating within a wisdom that will honor my vulnerability. Trusting in God means also trusting in the natural processes that carry me along through life. I no longer expect to be protected from them by miraculous intervention, but I hope to become more heroic in responding in trust and creativity to whatever my life brings along. The way the world functions within the laws of the Cosmos will hurt us, but it will also bring us—along with the rest of the Universe—up to the heights of fulfillment where our destiny lies.

HUMAN MISTAKES

Trusting in the world is necessary if human beings are to live with integrity and honor. When we lose touch with the trustworthy nature of existence, we make many mistakes. We become hostile and grasping in our efforts to find security: "We repress the sense of being organically encompassed by a trustworthy process infinitely larger and more important than ourselves. We lose touch somehow with reality as we feel it in primary perception."[4] When we lose trust, we begin to act badly: the Universe becomes our enemy, we become afraid and aggressive, we grasp at life in the hope that we will find security, we put ourselves individually above the whole.

Much of the suffering in the world is not simply the result of the laws of nature, but is caused by human beings. A cursory sweep of the current suffering of humanity and the rest of the Earth community brings to mind the violence of war, the sting of injustice and prejudice, the pangs of starvation due to the unequal sharing of resources, the ache of dire poverty, the smear of pollution, the destruction of animal species, the trampling of the environment—need I go on? We are all more than familiar with this endless list. Myopic, self-protectionist human practices have mired the planet in unnecessary agony.

All of this does not mean that humans are simply greedy megalomaniacs who do not care about the Earth, but it points more to their vulnerability and their urgent need for self-protection within a frighten-

4. Ibid., chap. 12, para. 4.

ing Universe. It is ironic that while their response to vulnerability causes more suffering, it also creates the impulse to try and stamp out pain in any form. Out of the depth of their fear, humans devote themselves to eradicating violence and destruction, and, of course, this causes more violence and destruction. An important insight of Berry and Swimme is that people, particularly those in the West, are determined to eliminate any kind of suffering, pain, struggle or limitation.[5] They say we rail against the human condition in its vulnerability to danger and its confinement within the natural contours of existence. We find it unacceptable that life keeps throwing chaos and suffering our way and so busy ourselves trying to fix everything so that we can live a pain-free existence. Whenever a disaster strikes, we scurry around, shoring up the walls of our many dikes, in the illusion that we can stop it from occurring again. On the news we hear that everything possible is being done "so that this will never happen again." Even discomfort bothers us, so we concentrate a large portion of our energy on inventing timesaving and comfort-inducing products that will create a kind of heaven on Earth. While some of this is necessary and positive, we seem to have gone overboard in trying to shut out anything remotely painful from our lives. This lifestyle has emerged from a lack of trust in the ways of nature and an inability to deal with life as it really is.

SIN AND EVIL

So far, we have been discussing the mistakes humans make from their reaction to fear. But what about what religion calls sin? What about the culpability the human race must accept for its choices to do harm? Is there a force of evil in the world that we have traditionally called the devil? Are there two realms, good and evil, in continual battle to win the hearts of human beings?

In my opinion, there is definitely evil in the world, but it is not caused by a force or by a devil. At its best, religion has always stated that evil arises from freedom. Theologians of every stripe tell us in different ways that God created the world free, so that it could choose love over hate, life over death. This had to be so because love cannot be love unless it is chosen. There is no coercion in love. In the Judeo-Christian tradition, evil is personified into Satan or the devil. As the story (which is a mixture of legends from the Middle East) goes, Satan was one of the most powerful

---

5. Berry and Swimme, *Universe Story*, 56.

angels, but he became so full of pride that he would no longer worship God and was cast out of heaven. His fall from heaven created hell, which was devoid of the presence of God and therefore the opposite of heaven, and from there he leads a rebellion, continually trying to lure humans away from obedience to God. This fascinating myth has unfortunately been concretized and used to terrify the masses into being good, but it is a powerful, insightful story that points to the absolute importance of making choices and bearing the consequences of them. Because Satan was free, he chose ego over love. The hell he created is not a place, but what happens to free creatures when they choose the path of death and 'unlove.' They lose themselves utterly. What we choose to do each moment of each day matters. It either moves the Universe forward to life or backwards to death.

What about the other pivotal story of the origin of human evil? I am referring to the Adam and Eve myth from the Hebrew bible, but there is a story like it in every culture on Earth. Deep in the human psyche there seems to be a sense that something is wrong and conflicted within the human heart. As St. Paul puts it, "For I do not do the good I want, but the evil I do not want is what I do."[6] This myth has received a wealth of interpretation, but I will simply share a few of the things it means and does not mean for me. It does not mean that God created a Universe/paradise without polarities, in which fully actualized people lived in perfect love, and then human beings ruined the whole thing by choosing to go against God's wishes. It does not mean that either the Universe or the human race is fallen and that humans must carry the burden of guilt for the suffering in the world. I believe that the Cosmos came into being as a seed which has been growing and maturing all the while until this present moment. Likewise, human beings were not perfect once and then fell into imperfection. They have been slowly evolving from a very primitive state, and indeed they are still very young and have much maturing to do. For me, the story simply points to the tension human beings feel about living up to their potential to become love. We know that we are on our way, but also that we have a long way to go to actualize the fullness of our humanity. Heroes like Mahatma Gandhi and Martin Luther King Jr. give us glimpses of the possibilities for human existence, but we struggle continually with the knowledge of our limitations and our unwillingness

6. Rom. 7:19 (NRSV).

to be transformed. There is a choice to be made every day: will we do our utmost to live in harmony with the Universe, or will we sink back into egotistical discord? Thankfully, we are not alone in our struggle. The lure of the Universe beckons us onward. Teilhard assures us that God is both propelling and drawing us into Omega. The communion of the saints is cheering us on. The story of Adam and Eve is not something that happened in the past, but it is a continuing chronicle of the consequences of choosing death over life. The Cosmos urges us: "Choose life."[7]

I have come to believe that there is no natural evil in the Cosmos, only goodness, only the divine energy of life and love that gave birth to it, sustains it, and fulfills it. This shines out like brilliant light, bathing all things in creativity, potential, beauty and wisdom. The darkness that we experience can only be caused by shadow. God's loving energy pours over all things all the time, and evil is the choice to live in the shadows. Evil is not a force but an absence of that which enlivens and completes us.

Brian Swimme says that 'good' is everything that leads the Universe to greater heights in its ongoing adventure, and that 'evil' is everything that diminishes the life of the Cosmos. Each day, we humans are invited to live in love, sensitivity, thoughtfulness, kindness, compassion, physical alacrity, mental sharpness, and spiritual depth. Each day, the radical freedom of choice that is ours allows us the possibility of causing evil by living in hate, insensitivity, thoughtlessness, selfishness, aggression, physical laziness, mental dullness, spiritual shallowness. There is no devil or force of darkness. There is only the one good world (which can cause us suffering but is not evil) and the light of divine love that pours upon everything at every moment.

If there is no force of evil luring us into sin, why do we have such a struggle choosing to live in the light? Most of us do not go around deliberately causing harm to others or to the environment, yet even with the best of intentions we have to make a huge effort to live up to our principles, and we seem to produce a mixed result. I know exactly what I should do to play my part in reducing my negative impact on nature, but I continually fight with my own laziness, thoughtlessness, greed, and selfishness. We come into this world with a raw package of human and individual traits and the freedom to make something of them, the freedom to respond or not to the love that surrounds us. The circumstances of our

7. Deut. 30:19 (NRSV).

lives can greatly affect our ability to grow in love, but all each one of us can do is make the most of what we have—we always still have our freedom. All the world's religions tell us that it is a life's work to discipline our appetites and tendencies and to gradually shift our focus away from our ego toward the wellbeing of others. We need all the help we can get from the practices they teach and the wisdom they impart. Most of all we need love itself to teach us how to become love. We need to open ourselves wide to the lure of the world's life energy. We need God.

THEODICY PROBLEM

There is no devil or force of evil to blame for the suffering of the world. This brings us back squarely to the perennial question: Why does the all-good God allow suffering in the world? This is a specifically religious question, but even taking God out of the picture, we are still left asking—if the energy and intelligence that shapes the world is beneficent, how can we explain the presence of so much misery? We look around ourselves and wonder how the world could be such an awful mess. We can blame human mistakes for a lot of it, but what about disease and natural disasters—are they acts of God? If they are, then it seems God does not care about human beings and all the other life forms that are affected. If they are just acts of nature, does this mean that the Earth, far from being our mother, is disinterested in the fate of its creatures? Consider the following assertion of Timothy Ferris: "Needless to say, science in itself will not deliver us from the dangers to which its knowledge has exposed us . . . If we plead with nature, it is in vain; she is wonderfully indifferent to our fate, and it is her custom to try everything and to be ruthless with incompetence. Ninety-nine percent of all the species that have lived on Earth have died away, and no stars will wink out in tribute if we in our folly soon join them."[8]

Ferris wrote this while reflecting on the present global environmental crisis. It chills me to the bone when I read it, and I can't help but agree that there is an uncompromising ruthlessness to the ways of the Universe. Richard Dawkins, who is famous for his atheism, wrote that nature is characterized by "blind, pitiless indifference."[9] I am reminded of the monstrous beast in W.B. Yeats's poem "The Second Coming," described

8. Ferris, *Whole Shebang*, 387.

9. Dawkins, *River Out of Eden*, 133.

as a "shape with lion body and the head of a man." It is a metaphor for intractable evil, its gaze "blank and pitiless as the Sun," an anti-Christ "slouch[ing] towards Bethlehem to be born."[10] Where is the caring God who worries about every hair on our heads? If there is a compassionate, loving creator, why did God make the world this way? If the ground of being is essentially love, then how can it produce such horror as the suffering of children? Why couldn't God have created another kind of Universe where suffering isn't so prevalent? How could love have produced such a "terrible beauty?"[11] Is there perhaps some other kind of world possible?

The ancient, unanswerable question always receives the same answer—which never suffices when agony strikes. Suffering is necessary so the world can be free to grow and develop toward its destiny. What other kind of Universe could there be? Without the possibility of suffering, there can be no real love because love involves choice and choice involves freedom.

But is nature really indifferent to the pain and the fate of its creatures? I have come to the conclusion, based on my own experience, that the processes of nature are kind as well as cruel. What taught me this, above anything that I have ever read or heard, was the experience of having a baby. I feel sure that pregnancy and childbirth have helped many women understand the nature of suffering. Having two children has increased my trust level; it has revealed to me the firm tenderness of nature which insists that we make the journey through all life's stages of labor so that we may continually grow and give birth to new aspects of our person. Nature is a very capable midwife who knows exactly what to do to ease her fearful charges through the painful struggles of birth. One of her tricks is to allow the passing of time to prepare us, step by step, for moments of great trial.

When I became pregnant with my first child, I was initially thrilled and, shortly afterward, terrified. The inevitability of having to go through childbirth filled me with anxiety and dread. My first trimester brought nausea and heartburn, and I felt so uncomfortable that I looked eagerly to the end of those three months for relief. Before I knew it, I was settled more deeply into the metamorphosis my body was going through, and I experienced the sense of being carried along by a process much wiser

10. Jeffares, W. B. Yeats, 99.

11. Ibid., 93.

and stronger than me. As time passed, and childbirth got closer, I became more and more reconciled to it until giving birth became the focus of my life. My pregnancy was not difficult by any means, just increasingly more uncomfortable as time went on. By the time my due date came, I just wanted to have the baby. I was ready. Yes, when the first labor pains started (three weeks early) I had a spasm of fear, but that passed quite quickly into concentrating on moving with the rhythms of my body. I just let nature carry me through.

Reflecting on the whole experience afterward, I realized that nature prepares us gradually for the inevitable stages of growth and decline that make up our sojourn through life. When my children feel afraid of events looming in the future, such as leaving home or the deaths of my husband and myself, I tell them that nature will prepare them to go through those trials in a gradual way. Leaving home will be eased by the call of adventure and independence; that same independence plus much growth and maturity will prepare them for our deaths. Nature teaches us how to go through pain and struggle, step by step, within the passing of time. Sometimes pain comes suddenly and disasters happen in an untimely fashion, but nature has other skills to get us through those times, like the numbness that shock produces and the amnesia that follows traumatic events. When it comes to our own deaths, which we fear so greatly, again nature eases us into the next realm, step by step, slowly and with sure hands. The competent midwife returns.[12]

Where is God when we suffer and die? God is in the natural processes that nurture and hold us and ease us through the stages of living and dying. God is in the consoling friend and compassionate family member. God feels pain with us. God is not the perfectly self-sufficient, aloof deity of some theologies, but the one who suffers along with creation. God is truly affected by our pains and joys because love is by definition relational. A love relationship necessarily involves empathetic presence to a loved one's feelings. God is not impassive and distant but shares fully in everything that we experience.

Again, the image of Jesus on the cross is of central significance to me. I have let go of many of the Church's assertions about Jesus, but I

---

12. Having said this, I am well aware that I am speaking from within the safe boundaries of a life that has not been rocked by the unthinkable traumas that beset many people. Some pain is simply unbearable and it is not my wish to offer platitudes that belittle terrible suffering.

deeply believe he is a manifestation of the heart of God. In Jesus I know love. How many Christians have held onto the cross as they were dying or enduring a painful trial, not because of theological notions of fall and redemption, but because it symbolized God's suffering with them? In my darkest hours, I return to this image because, when nothing at all makes sense, I experience through it not only God's compassion but also a promise—that love triumphs over hate, that life is stronger than death, that nothing in the end is lost, and all is harvest. It gives me hope.

9

Wrestling with God

THERE IS A STORY in the Bible that offers a perfect allegory for this chapter. Allow me to tell it.

One evening, the patriarch Jacob, who was not shy about getting blessings out of life, was alone, when a man (some translations say an angel) appeared who wrestled with him all night long. It seems that Jacob knew that the one he wrestled with was no ordinary human, and he was determined to get all that he could out of this fight. He hung onto his adversary for dear life and would not concede defeat even when he was wounded so badly that he would limp for the rest of his life. At daybreak the man insisted that Jacob let go of him for neither of them could win the fight, but Jacob said, "I will not let you go, unless you bless me." After asking his name and being told it was Jacob, the man said, "You shall no longer be called Jacob, but Israel, for you have striven with God and with humans, and you have prevailed." Jacob received his blessing from the mysterious stranger who would not reveal his name, and he dedicated the battle site as sacred, saying that he had seen God face to face and had lived.[1]

This was obviously a life-changing experience for Jacob as his name change indicates. Jacob means supplanter or deceiver, which refers to the fact that he stole his brother Esau's birthright, while Israel means champion of God. Wrestling with God was cathartic for Jacob and prepared him for the critical role he was to play in the history of his people. However, the relationship of Israel the person and Israel the nation to God was never smooth or polite, but continued to be characterized by wrestling and struggle. Elohim, as God was known, never became meek and mild, and Israel never became pious and pliable, and therefore, their

1. Gen. 32:24–30 (NRSV).

story is paradigmatic of life as it happens. If we wish to receive the blessings that life can bring, we should not expect a comfortable ride but an epic journey full of the triumphs and devastations of true adventure. We have to wrestle with God in order to be fully alive and fulfilled. When bad things happen, as they surely will in this world of yin-yang polarities, it does us no good to blame God and sit in a heap of passive misery. Better to scream our pain at God and wrestle with life until it yields its blessing from the heart of suffering.

I have never been strong and heroic like this, but I am beginning to see the sense in it. I am beginning to feel the stirrings of courage within. A good friend of mine has a phrase that he used to repeat to me often, probably because he could see I was such a wimp. He would say, "You cannot afford the luxury of self-pity." I am only now starting to understand the depth of this wisdom. Like Jacob, we have to struggle with life and be wounded by it, so that even though we limp, we become blessed by ever-increasing wholeness and aliveness, so that we can penetrate the mystery of losing ourselves to find ourselves. In order to receive God's blessings we must struggle, take risks, ride the currents, fall down and get up again, scream, and rage when life hurts us too much. If we are fully engaged with the adventure of our lives, no matter what it throws at us, we will be blessed. Being blessed by life means discovering our destiny and achieving our potential. There is no other way to be successful in this life. It is the very struggle that brings out the best in us. Even though we will suffer through nights of pain we will find, at dawn, new strength, deeper wisdom, increased capacity to become love. Love is not only gentle; it is also tough. God is not only kind, but also demanding.

Why did Jacob have to wrestle with God in order to be blessed? Is it not true that God pours out blessings on all creation in a continuous unearned, undeserved stream? That is the definition of grace, which describes the generous, unconditional nature of love. What this story teaches us is not that God is stingy with blessings, but that struggle is a necessary part of the process of receiving blessings. We cannot grow unless we face and overcome difficulties. Life is not about passivity but activity and choice. Jacob wrestled through the night and was hurt in the struggle with the mysterious stranger, but through this ordeal he regained a sense of his identity and destiny and touched ultimate reality. He received the blessings that he was prepared to fight for.

STORIES OF LIFE

Have you ever noticed that great adventures only seem glorious at their beginning and end? What happens in the middle is often far from thrilling, and we tend to lose sight of the high ideals that motivated us in the first place. In Tolkien's *Lord of the Rings*, the hobbits from the Shire allowed themselves to be stirred out of their habitual comfort by the lure of high adventure, but when they were deep in Mordor, Sam and Frodo wondered how they could have agreed to such a journey and wished themselves safe home in bed.

It is fascinating to me how good stories reflect the drama that is played out in every human life. The traditional plot always revolves around the rise and resolution of conflict, how it is dealt with, and what lessons are learned through the process. This came home to me in a powerful way recently when I watched a documentary series about two actors, Ewan McGregor and Charley Boorman, who decided to try to ride their motorbikes on a 20,000-mile journey across the longest continuous landmass on Earth, through the Ukraine, Kazakhstan, Mongolia, China, Siberia, Alaska, and Canada before arriving in the United States.[2] The actors co-produced their story and decided to give a daily running commentary throughout their adventure. This device allows the audience a window into their feelings about the ups and downs of the trip, and it soon becomes evident that the series is more about the participants than the scenery. It gradually takes on the characteristics of a good story where Ewan and Charley are the protagonists in a drama with all the usual elements: exposition, introduction of conflict, rising action, climax, falling action and resolution. The fact that the two are actors and that they offer their reflections on the ongoing story adds irony and extra layers to the whole adventure.

The exposition in *The Long Way Round* introduces the characters and the plan for the big trip. Personally, I was bored at this stage and did not know whether I would continue to watch or not. The first few episodes are mildly entertaining; the roads are pretty good and the places they visit quite interesting. Then the conflict begins, and the rising action takes a sharp turn toward riveting when the tarmac runs out and the bikers find themselves on increasingly difficult roads in isolated countryside. The drama intensifies as they enter the Road of Bones (in far eastern

2. Boorman and McGregor, *Long Way Round*.

Russia, built by Stalin using labor camp and gulag prisoners whose bones became incorporated into the road), which is primitive, muddy, and so rutted that they can barely stay on their bikes for more than a few yards at a time. They need every ounce of strength and endurance to keep picking up their bikes and continuing on. One of the bikes breaks down, and their crew van has an accident. Some of the crew members voice the opinion that a joy ride is not worth all the pain, effort and mounting danger they are experiencing. The bikers themselves are increasingly exhausted but undaunted by the difficulties. The trip becomes something that they must complete—a test of their courage and mettle, an opportunity to wrestle with life. Both men are on the verge of entering middle age and acknowledge that the main reason for this adventure is to push the boundaries of their lives past the impasse of staleness and predictability. The conflict of their story is between the protagonist, the human spirit (personified by Ewan and Charley), and the antagonist, nature, and it is obvious they these men are utterly respectful and awe-filled by the power and beauty of their foe. Their commentary gives witness to how deeply moved they are by their surroundings. When the trip is over they pine after these roads like a sailor on dry land.

The climax of the story comes when the adventurers must cross a virtually impassable river where the bridge has been washed out, in order to reach the good roads and relative comfort on the other side. It is a do-or-die situation. They cannot go back and must find a way forward. After much waiting and desperate deliberation, they eventually manage to catch a ride over the river aboard one of the huge trucks that transport goods along this treacherous road. The only way over is to plough into the water and force their way up the other bank. This is accomplished with much heart-stopping rocking, tipping, and swaying, but the beast manages to spin and screech its way to the other side. For a while, Ewan and Charley are euphoric and taste the triumph of difficulties overcome. They celebrate, sleep off some of their exhaustion, and continue on their journey, which is now a relative cakewalk. But now the action falls precipitously. As they ride on beautiful, paved roads for the rest of their trip, they cannot really enjoy the scenery and comfort because they long to be back wrestling with God on the Road of Bones. The audience feels the same nostalgia for high adventure, and it is hard to sustain any interest in the final leg of the trip. The resolution of all the problems is a letdown rather than a 'happy ever after.'

The end of the series left me pondering two curiosities: the contrary nature of human beings and the compelling nature of story. How curious it is that humans tend to choose the path of least resistance and long for pleasure, comfort and ease, when it is the exact opposite of these that gives them the most satisfaction and joy. In *The Long Way Round*, by far the most memorable part of the trip was the most difficult. Ewan and Charley felt themselves to be most alive when they were physically exhausted, roughing it in enormous discomfort, and facing problem after problem on the road. The situation brought out aspects of their personalities that they did not know were there—or were not sure were still there after years of comfortable hibernation. Facing and overcoming adversity seems to bring out the best in human beings. Crisis awakens our creativity. Wrestling with God reveals to us our true identity, our possibilities, and our destinies. Without the challenges and difficulties of our lives, we would never discover who we are and who we could become.

Stories are so compelling and captivating because they mirror back to us the central drama of our own lives. The structure of drama from exposition to resolution is the shape of our inner world as we confront (or run away from) the struggles and conflicts of our own personal adventures. The challenges we face from day to day may be very minor or excruciatingly major, but how we deal with them reveals our strengths and inadequacies. It calls forth our fortitude or our cowardice, our ingenuity or our dullness; it causes us to grow or diminish; it teaches us to reach higher or settle for the status quo. The choice is ours, but we keep seeking out the stories because they contain our own possibilities. We are fascinated with conflict even as we seek to avoid it.

THE NECESSITY OF STRUGGLE

Facing and overcoming adversity makes us feel alive; indeed, it brings us greater life. If we stay as safe as possible, we don't reach the limits of our potential or receive what life wants to gift us with. We are in danger of living a quiet, unlived life. That was certainly my temptation when I decided never to marry and have children. I saw all the pain and difficulties that were part of married life, all the disasters that might occur, the high stakes involved in trusting my life to one person, and I figured it would be much more prudent to stay out of those dangerous waters. Making the choice to marry and bring children into this scary world was a huge leap into adventure for me. At this time I had a poster on my wall that gave me courage; it was a picture of a ship at full sail following a strong headwind and it read, "Ships are safe in the harbor, but that is not what ships are for." I suppose that has become a trite image now, but it still speaks volumes to me.

To those outside our inner circle our lives may look very ordinary and perhaps boring, but only we, and those close to us, know the drama that goes on under the surface of our seemingly calm seas. Probably the biggest adversary in my life at present is writing this book. It has taken me years to get to this point in my writing—and I am not a patient person. I have nearly given up hundreds of times. A steady stream of comments from my inner critic buzzes around my brain every time I try to write: Why on Earth are you putting yourself through this hard work? Nobody will publish it. Who do you think you are writing a book—some kind of expert? You don't write very well—your book sounds like a high school essay. No one will be interested in reading this kind of stuff; it is cliché now; better writers than you have already covered this material. And on it goes. Yet, I can't seem to put a halt to this project, because I know I need it to grow.

The point I am trying to make here is that we need some chaos, conflict, and struggle in our lives. They cause us to suffer, but they call us to growth. Sometimes we choose our challenges and sometimes, often, they choose us. Most of the time, we do not need to go looking for trouble—indeed it would be foolish to do so—it finds us quite easily on its own. As we have seen, life is so structured, between the polarities of chaos and determinism, that one thing we can be sure of is the presence of difficulty and its ensuing suffering in our lives. I am arguing here that we need to find a way to respond creatively to the 'bad' things that happen. Inside each conflict situation is a possibility, a promise. If we can bear with our grief and pain, we will find the golden key that lies in the bottom of our casket of suffering and unlock the door to greater life. This is all part of the process of learning to love. Loving always eventually means losing. It leads us on a painful and glorious journey, but if we have the courage to stay on this path, we will, as Kahlil Gibran tells us, laugh all our laughter and cry all our tears.[3]

3. Gibran, *The Prophet*, 12.

CREATIVE ENGAGEMENT WITH THE ENEMY

As usual, our friend Brian Swimme provides much inspiration to us in our quest for the fullness of life. He tells us that we cannot achieve happiness by protecting ourselves. He says that in our attempt to live in a safe bubble, "we have done away with many of the most delightful and creative aspects of our existence . . . Death and pain are necessary for deep adventure, and our existence would be mediocre without it."[4] Swimme suggests that we call all the things in life that cause us pain and struggle "the enemy," and he insists that we have a fundamental need for worthy opponents. The reason for this is that enemies awaken our creativity and release our energy: "Our creativity demands our enemy. Your enemy is where your energy is. If you don't have an enemy, you don't have energy."[5]

All of nature operates on this principle. Resistance shapes the Cosmos. For instance, the atom is created out of the resistance of the electron and the proton; the entire Universe would collapse if the resistance was overcome. There are many examples of the central part that resistance plays in the natural world. Swimme speaks of the relationship between the hawk and the mouse. One is the hunter and the other the hunted, but they both owe their special gifts to the resistance created by their interaction. The hawk has razor sharp eyesight and can plummet huge distances from the sky to the ground with incredible swiftness. These attributes are what give the bird its magnificence. However, these same gifts are dependent upon the tiny creatures it feeds on. The hawk developed such elegance because mice are so difficult to catch. Mice have the advantage of being small, camouflaged, excellent hiders and fast movers. Being the prey of hawks provoked the emergence of these attributes. The resistance in this relationship allowed both creatures to develop their potential. Each found a worthy opponent in the other.[6]

Who or what is the enemy? Where is it? Naming our enemies can be a tricky thing, because while they seem to be outside of ourselves, their roots are often inside of us. I may discover that the tremendous anger I feel against a fellow worker is provoked by my own insecurities. The enemy can be a person, a disease, an event, a country; in fact, it is anything or anybody that causes us to suffer. The way we respond to our enemies

4. Swimme, *Canticle to Cosmos*, 7.

5. Ibid., 5.

6. Ibid., 5.

is critical because, as Brian Swimme says, "The enemy has a secret. The secret is ourselves."[7]

There are two mistakes we can make in dealing with our enemies: we can either aggressively crush them or we can passively ignore them. Both of these are unhealthy, unproductive responses that always make matters worse not better. The elimination of resistance is not helpful, nor is passivity to it. As we have already seen, the Western response to the enemy has historically been one of aggression. We try to obliterate the opposition.

The extreme example of warfare offers a clear demonstration of this uncreative response to the enemy. The United States does not have the monopoly on aggression, but the current situation of widespread warfare following the 9/11 disaster allows us to see this principle in operation. After the awful events of September 11, 2001, there seemed to be no attempt on the part of the American nation to engage in serious reflection on the causes of this terrible violence. A few voices tried to suggest that past and present American foreign policy might have played a part in the eruption of hatred towards the U.S., but these brave souls were considered traitorous by the government. Neither was there any attempt to engage the enemy creatively in any kind of negotiation. Instead, the crisis was painted as a war between good and evil, with all the evil projected well away from the home front. In his Address to the Nation after 9/11, President Bush said, "America was targeted for attack because we're the brightest beacon for freedom and opportunity in the world. And no one will keep that light from shining."[8] This introduces biblical images of light and darkness. He referred to America's enemies as the Axis of Evil. The following War on Terror has entailed the full force of the American military trying to obliterate 'evil.' This rhetoric is by no means one-sided, as it also fuels the passion of Islamic fundamentalists, who see themselves as champions of goodness fighting to destroy the evil perversions of the Western world. No matter what we think of who is wrong or right in this unholy mess, it is clear that both sides are intent on the obliteration of the enemy and that this approach is bringing nothing but more violence and hatred to our world. Although Brian Swimme said the following words

7. Ibid., 5.
8. Bush, "Address to Nation," para. 3.

long before 9/11, he has been proven prophetic in his insight: "The great-est evil in our day is caused by those who wish to obliterate evil."[9]

What about the other mistaken approach to resistance—passivity and denial? We all know the terrible tension and chaos that can build up in our lives when we refuse to deal with the problems and difficulties life sends our way. Molehills gradually become mountains and the mountains loom large, casting a heavy shadow over everything else. Conversely, inat-tention to painful realities can cause dissipation and decay. For instance, a marriage cannot survive if one or both partners refuse to engage in the necessary confrontation that brings growth and resolution of is-sues; it will eventually fizzle out or become a shadow of a real marriage. Repression of unpleasant emotions and denial of problems can result in depression or anxiety. Passivity not only brings disease of the mind and spirit, it dramatically curtails the adventure each life should be and many opportunities to grow are wasted.

As unpleasant and sometimes devastating as it can be, crisis is neces-sary to bring forth the deepest creativity of the human race. It has often been pointed out that the Chinese translation of the word *crisis* contains the notions of both danger and opportunity. The Greek meaning of the word is *moment of decision.* So, while crisis has the potential for terrible disaster, its power to awaken the utmost inventiveness within the human psyche offers the opportunity for the wholesale flowering of human gift-edness. Of course, crises can be handled badly, as we have seen, but they often bring out the best in us. Compassion and generosity stir in people's hearts; ordinary life breaks open allowing depth of reflection and creativ-ity of action to emerge; spirituality awakens with the need to see beyond narrow horizons. It is ironic that only true crisis can bring forth the solu-tions to the world's most urgent problems. The problems themselves pro-voke their own resolution. It seems as if humans resist change until they realize that disaster will fall on their heads if they do not do something. Witness the current crisis of climate change that is finally penetrating the thick skull of global consciousness. A surge of creativity is building momentum that will not only address climate change but the whole range of ecological problems that the planet faces. It took, in my opinion, the destructive raging storms and the life-sucking droughts of the last couple of years to bring the message home to the world's human population.

---

9. Swimme, *Canticle to Cosmos*, 5.

Weather experts and scientists can say all they want but nothing prods us out of denial faster than feeling the bite of climate change firsthand. The trouble is, we have the habit of sliding back into our life-as-normal rut as soon as we think trouble has passed. If humans hope to solve the urgent ecological problems they have caused, it is imperative that they embrace crisis and be actively engaged with the enemy of environmental damage. The clock is ticking, and we do not have much time left to avoid terrible disaster.

Finding the balance between obliterating the enemy and ignoring it is key to finding a healthy response to life's difficulties. The story of Jacob wrestling with God offers a great paradigm for this. It teaches us that it is possible to struggle with the enemy and embrace it at the same time. This paradoxical striving awakens our deepest levels of creativity and causes enormous quantities of energy to be released, which is necessary, both to overcome problems and also to further the great adventure of life. Swimme calls this creative engagement. The dynamics of life demand that we wrestle creatively with our enemies, both without and within, and then we will be granted the blessing that we seek and discover both our identity and our destiny.

10

Forging Beauty

HAVE YOU EVER MET a beautiful person? I don't mean simply a physically beautiful person, but one who attracts everyone around him or her and remains warmly and pleasurably in the memory. People like that inspire a kind of longing, a desire to be whole because they radiate a harmony that speaks of the rich synthesis they have forged from the disparate forces of their lives and personalities. Their beauty is not superficial but comes from a profound place where the pleasures of life have been drunk deeply yet carefully, and the misfortunes of existence have been embraced heroically. They have achieved beauty as a creative response to cosmic suffering, taking the pain of life and forging it into a work of art. Creatively engaging the enemy has won them their blessings. Beautiful people are heroes who have achieved the art of balancing with dexterity on the knife-edge of life. They are artists and acrobats who became beautiful through disciplined training and creative exploration. Beauty radiates from their creations and from their persons. In the language of science, one could say that beautiful people have found the safe passage between the crushing forces of chaos and determinism and emerged whole.

ANOTHER FINE BALANCE

Beauty in human beings and the Cosmos is the product of the Universe's orientation toward chaos in tension with its movement toward order. Chaos is always churning up a storm, creating the possibility for continual novelty to emerge. Determinism, or order, is forever smoothing the waters and stabilizing raw energy into symmetry and elegance. Beauty is dependent on both forces. This is simply the way the Universe is. It is startling to think that there could have been any number of universes in existence, consisting of elements that would make them very different from our own home. For all we know there could be other universes around right now that we know nothing about and are nothing like the one that we have become accustomed to. What is clear is that our own Universe operates on particular principles that orient it in a certain direction. Our Cosmos is shaped in such a way that chaos and determinism produce beauty. I am not simply speaking of the violent clash of cosmic properties, but of a teleological dimension. Beauty emerges as the very aim of the Universe and the goal of existence.

Alfred North Whitehead wrote about beauty this way.[1] He considered it to be the highest value that the Cosmos constantly strained toward. According to Whitehead, beauty is caused by the harmonizing of the opposite poles of chaos and uniformity, or novelty and order, neither of which can produce anything but ugliness when taken in isolation. By itself, order is monotonous and uncreative; chaos is rich in possibility but also dangerously destructive, and it cannot produce beauty unless it is harmonized with the stabilizing forces of order. John Haught tells us, "The beautiful is threatened on two sides, by chaos on one side and monotony or triviality on the other. Beauty is a balancing act between the extremes of chaos and banality."[2] The greater the complexity involved in this synthesis, the more intense the beauty that is achieved. Therefore, the Universe, which is growing in complexity according to its evolutionary path, has the capacity to achieve ever-increasing states of beauty. To imagine that beauty is the aim of all existence is a little confusing and perhaps even disappointing to our Western philosophical sensibilities. We are far more used to ethical principles taking the top billing in our world's values. To be good has always been our highest aim, and being beautiful has been relegated to the sidelines as rather unimportant and superficial. However, this is due to an impoverished understanding of what beauty is.

WHAT IS BEAUTY?

Surprisingly enough, science has a lot to say about the nature of beauty. Through a close study of the Cosmos, scientists propose that beauty is not just a property of the human mind, but actually an integral part of nature. It is the guide and standard by which a scientific theory is deemed to be true. Time and again scientific experimentation confirms that what

1. Whitehead, *Adventures of Ideas*, 265.
2. Haught, *Cosmic Adventure*, chap. 8, para. 11.

is true is what is beautiful. Einstein's theory of relativity was received enthusiastically in the science world because of the simplicity and beauty
of its equations. Mathematicians speak of the elegance of formulas, and
biologists speak of the symmetry of the natural world. Scientists ascribe
three attributes to beauty: simplicity, harmony, and clarity. To be beauti-
fully simple, a theory needs to be complete, with nothing lacking, but also
economical, with nothing superfluous added. Harmony speaks of balance
and symmetry. The symmetrical laws of physics reflect the balance found
in nature. Einstein went so far as to say that science could not exist if there
were no intrinsic harmony in the Cosmos itself. Clarity is an essential
aspect of beauty because the beautiful is not only radiant in itself, it sheds
light all around, illuminating and making connections between associated phenomena. Beauty is not just in the human mind, it is a natural
aspect of the Universe.[3] Perhaps it would be clearer to say that beauty is in
the human mind because it is a property of nature.

The old saying "Beauty is in the eye of the beholder" takes on new
meaning when considered within the insights of the new cosmology. We
say that turquoise lakes and forests of autumn maples are beautiful. So
are cashmere sweaters and Tchaikovsky symphonies. This is so because
all of our senses, our organs of perception, are completely attuned to the
world from which we ourselves emerged. We evolved very slowly from
the stars—no wonder we resonate with creation and find nature so over-
whelmingly gorgeous. All of it is kin to us. Religious thinkers say that
God, from whom all existence flows, is the ultimate in perfect beauty, and
so all creatures and entities reflect the loveliness of the divine. But wait a
minute—aren't there things in the world that we find ugly and repellent?
What about rotting carcasses, grimy back alleys, or gardens overrun with
weeds? Why do we find these ugly? I suppose one could say that not only
beauty is in the eye of the beholder, but ugliness too. Where does that
come from? We are back to the world of yin and yang, polarized opposites,
creative tension, looking once more for the balance in things. Perhaps
things are ugly to us when chaos overcomes order—or vice versa.

Whitehead suggests that we find things beautiful when a balance between chaos and uniformity has been established. Unpacking this, Haught
says that "we call beautiful any expression, entity or experience that trans-

---

3. Augros and Stanciu, *New Story*, 37–50.

forms or resolves contradictions into contrasts."[4] Contrast seems to be the key word. In art, we are drawn to works that offer depth of contrast and the creative synthesis of novelty and harmony. A work that tips over into clashing discord may interest us, but it is difficult to call it beautiful. A piece that slides into monotony may seem pretty for a while, but we soon tire of its superficiality. We only find beautiful, works that both unsettle and attract us.

One of the reasons we find things to be ugly or boring is that we cannot always achieve a broad enough perspective to grasp the harmonizing of contradictions. Our perception of beauty is limited by our narrow vision. We are aware of only one minute aspect of an overarching reality. We can't see the wood for the trees, as the saying goes. If we imagine the world as one huge, exquisitely beautiful canvas painted by the divine cosmic artist, then it becomes clear that it will never be possible for us limited human beings to be able to appreciate the magnificence of the whole. To begin with, it is an ongoing project and not all the contradictions have been harmonized yet, and furthermore, we might be staring in despair into the black hole of one corner of the piece without being able to see that this is balanced by the brilliant radiance of a contrasting color close by.[5] It reminds me of watching television news, which purports to capture what is happening on the planet, but usually presents only the ugliest parts, leaving the viewer disheartened by the impression that the world is a terrible place. Only by seeing the whole canvas can one appreciate the beauty achieved by the harmonizing elements and contrasts. Only by having the broadest possible perspective of life on Earth can anyone judge its beauty or ugliness.

THE NEED FOR HEROES

We began this reflection on the nature of beauty by exploring the qualities that make a person beautiful. Human beings, gifted with the radical freedom of choosing their own response to life, are in the privileged position of being able to create beauty within their own personalities. Nature gives us a certain package, but we can determine what we will do with our particularities and shape who we will become. Life presents us with opportunities for growth, but it takes a lot of courage to become beautiful.

4. Haught, *Cosmic Adventure*, chap. 8, para. 10.

5. Ibid., chap. 8, para. 13.

In fact only heroes can achieve it. Heroes of all kinds are very beautiful people who have managed to harmonize the opposing elements of chaos and monotony. Haught tell us that heroism is beautiful "because it is the result of integrating a multiplicity of contrasting experiences (strength and frustration, joy and tragedy, rebellion and resignation, life and death) into the unity of a single person's story."[6]

It takes a certain kind of hero to deal with the forces of chaos that threaten to destabilize and annihilate order. Chaos can come in the form of the destroyer that tears apart the fabric of stability, smashing everything and everyone in its path. Some of its names are war, violence, catastrophe, and death. It can also come as the whirlwind that blows freshness, novelty, and excitement into any receptive heart. Some of its names are adventure, dreaming, change, and new life. In both forms, chaos can knock a person off balance, either staggering from the pain of attack, or free-falling from an excess of adventure. Neither form can achieve harmony and beauty. Some people love chaos, novelty, and excitement and chase the high experience. Their risk-taking can be destructive. These people crave continual stimulation and change in an unbalanced way.

What does it mean to be a hero when confronted with an overload of chaos? It means reaching deep into the peace that order, calm, and stillness can give to us. We are sometimes like over-stimulated or traumatized infants who need to be held close by their mothers and suck the life-giving comfort of their presence. It is strange how it takes great discipline to just stop and sit still. In times of great chaos we need to deliberately search out experiences that will lead us to the quiet waters of peace. In the stillness of meditation or contemplation, or perhaps in the understanding of a wise friend, we will come to an awareness that we need chaos in our lives so that we can grow and find ourselves, but that beauty comes from harmonizing its pressures with stability, depth, and emptiness.

It also takes heroism to contend with the forces of order that threaten to smother and deaden every spark of vitality they come across. Order can come in the form of the authoritarian who stamps on fresh ideas and threatens death either from violence or sheer boredom. Some of its names are prejudice, totalitarianism, conformity, and monotony. It can also come as the stabilizer, who calms fraught nerves, organizes mess, applies common sense to wild speculation, and makes rules to follow. Neither form

6. Ibid., chap. 8, para. 19.

can bring beauty on its own. Some people are tempted to the imbalance of monotony, stunting their growth through fear of risk-taking, or holding onto power by closing their minds to newness.

What does it mean to be a hero when faced with an excess of order? Sometimes it means being a rebel, such as the unlikely hero of the movie *Life is Beautiful (La vita è bella)*, co-written, directed, and performed in by Roberto Benigni.[7] Set in the closing year of World War II, this deeply moving, black comedy is about the refusal of one imprisoned Jewish man to bend to the crushing force of dehumanizing determinism. He rebels by maintaining his individualism, his sense of humor, and his love of life. Our hero hides his young son with him in the concentration camp and refuses to allow him to experience the hate machine of Nazism. He creates an imaginative world of hope, gentleness, and humor for his son, which has the audience laughing and crying at the same time. It is a truly extraordinary film. Even though the father does not make it to the end of the war, his son emerges intact because of the beautiful life that was created for him in the eye of the storm.

Sometimes, finding our balance against an overbearing monotony means being heroic in the face of soul-destroying sameness. Most of us have more trouble dealing with the monotony of our lives than with the threat of chaos or adversity. Working at the same job for thirty years or so, or going through the same routines day in and day out can make us feel, sometimes, as if we are barely alive. There are countless everyday heroes all around the world who manage to find beauty in life through a careful balance of persistence and creativity. It takes courage to persevere with a chosen life and not run away when boredom and monotony strike. It means seeking out the newness within the routines and taking delight in times of uniqueness and release.

Humans need to work hard at forging beauty out of the grist of their lives because they are in a very privileged position in the Universe. Brian Swimme recognizes the unique, cutting-edge place humans hold in the evolution of beauty. The Cosmos, in its ceaseless quest for ever- more intense expressions of beauty, has produced creatures who have an increasing capability of both creating and experiencing its beauty. Human beings, in the complexity of their self-reflexive consciousness are the creatures most suited to this task: "The history of life can be understood as

7. Cerami and Benigni, *Life is Beautiful.*

the creation of ever more sensitive creatures in a Universe where there is always another dimension of beauty to be felt and savored."[8] Swimme regards us as those creatures who can appreciate the beauty of the Universe most fully; indeed, he says that we are the Universe delighting in its own beauty. Our truest vocation is to journey ever more deeply into beauty by striving to balance the forces of chaos and determinism. We do this by becoming more finely tuned to the reality that we swim in: "We are awash with the presence of the Universe, already swamped in its beauty. All things have discharged themselves into the world, merely awaiting our development of the sensitivity to respond to them. To live as a mature human being is to journey home, and our home is enchantment."[9]

When Swimme refers to the possibility of humans resonating with reality, he speaks of developing our subjectivity—the sensitivity and depth which every person is capable of, but which needs nurturing and deliberate choice to develop. It is truly heroic to develop subjectivity because it involves exposing ourselves to great pain. Swimme contends (along with all the great mystics down through the ages) that if we could be open and receptive to all of reality as it is, we would be completely overwhelmed and shattered. We could not absorb such heightened beauty, but it is our destiny to expand our awareness as much as possible. Swimme asks if we can bear the pain of such a vision, yet the highest vocation of human beings is to choose depth, sensitivity, and openness to the dreadful beauty of all that is.

The world is a violent, destructive, gorgeous, thrilling place. Human beings are thrust into an existence where they must tread the knife-edge between chaos and determinism, trying to forge beauty and happiness from the raw material these two energies gift them with (even force upon them). The successful life means finding that fine balance between them. We are caught between the wild winds of chaos, which draw us out on a ledge and blow change, novelty, and adventure into our exposed faces, and the soft embrace of determinism, which lures us into the television den with its promise of safety and security. Just how will we respond to this dangerous, adventurous Universe?

8. Swimme, *Universe is Green Dragon*, 78–80.
9. Ibid., 95.

JESUS AND BEAUTY

The one who stands above others for me as a beautiful, heroic person is Jesus of Nazareth. As a man and as a sacrament of God, Jesus and his message have always thrilled me and drawn me into the heart of life's purpose and meaning. When I am able to connect with Jesus beyond the Church's excessive moralizing and obsessive worrying about sin and redemption, I have an emotional and noetic sense that I am touching ultimate reality. No doubt, this is because I was fortunate enough as a child to be enveloped within a truly nourishing, pervasive Catholic world that impressed itself indelibly on my heart and mind. This has always been my path up the mountain of God; there are many others, but it is a well-worn, reliable track. Sometimes, it appears to get lost in pernicious weeds or sickly flowers, but there always seems to be a rocky outcrop where it stands out bold and strong again. When I rediscover it, I feel at home again.

It seems a fitting conclusion to this look at cosmic suffering to dwell for a while on Jesus as the one who embodies the possibilities and potential of human beauty. His relationship with God was so intimate that he was a clear conduit of the beautiful divine presence. This bestowed upon him an irresistible authority, which allowed him to carve out a radically new vision of reality from the ancient rock of religion, taking human evolution a giant step forward. The wisdom and generosity that flows from this timeless figure offers abundant forgiveness for our mistakes, teaches us to engage creatively with our enemies, and restores our trust in the primacy of love.

Again, I am tremendously indebted to John Haught for his wonderful insights into the beauty of Jesus. He writes, in *The Cosmic Adventure*, that the great attraction of Jesus and his message is their tremendous beauty, caused by the integration of opposites into an intensely deep and harmonious synthesis.[10] Jesus maintains an exquisite balance between the forces of chaos and determinism and thus forges a new way that humans can become beautiful, can become fully human, can become one with God.

During his thirty some years in a repressed land in an obscure corner of the then-known world, Jesus led a revolution which shocked, upset, and delighted first the inhabitants of Palestine, and eventually the whole world. At the core of his new vision was a very ancient seed that had yet

10. Haught, *Cosmic Adventure*, chap. 12, para. 7.

to truly germinate in human society: that all people are equally important in the eyes of God and that each one is loved unconditionally. Jesus
embraced all people: tax collectors or the social elite, women or men,
children or adults, the healthy or the sick, rich or poor, pure or impure.
He accepted dinner invitations from the influential wealthy, whether they
were impressed with him or simply wanted to discredit him, but he was
just as happy to hang out with poor fishermen, social outcastes of various types, and even women, even menstruating women when necessary.
His acceptance of the people around him was total and unconditional,
and from this flowed their physical and spiritual healing. Jesus lived and
preached a compassion that subverted inequality and injustice. As exem-
plary Jesus scholar Marcus Borg states, "For Jesus, compassion was . . . a
social paradigm, the core value for life in community. To put it boldly:
compassion for Jesus was political. He directly and repeatedly challenged
the dominant sociopolitical paradigm of his social word and advocated
instead what might be called a politics of compassion."[11] Jesus was a mas-
ter of reconciling opposites.

Not only does the behavior of Jesus reveal the integration of polarities, but his stories function in the same way. As Haught tells us, his
parables reveal "a father embracing a prodigal son, a tax collector praying
for forgiveness; a heretic showing a compassion far surpassing that of the
orthodox, an employer rewarding laggards with the same wages as those
who have worked a full day."[12] In the parable of the mustard seed and others like it, Jesus proclaims that the greatest of all things, the kingdom of
God, grows from the tiniest beginning—something as insignificant and
commonplace as a mustard seed.[13]

The parable of the weeds in the wheat shows that the kingdom of
God, which is a symbol "for the deepest possible harmony of contrasts"
can only be achieved by the reconciling of opposites, not the aggressive
annihilation of the enemy.[14] The parable tells of a field of wheat that has
been deliberately sown with weeds by an enemy. The owner decides not
to pull up the weeds because he knows that the wheat will be uprooted
also and so tells his workers to let the weeds and the wheat grow side

11. Borg, *Meeting Jesus*, 49.

12. Haught, *Cosmic Adventure*, chap. 12, para. 7.

13. Mark 4:30–34 (NRSV).

14. Haught, *Cosmic Adventure*, chap. 12, para. 8.

by side until the harvest when they will be separated.[15] The evil in the world, represented by the weeds, is not removed from the good, which is represented by the wheat. The enemy is not destroyed because of the realization that good and evil are intimately rooted together and to destroy one would ultimately destroy the other. Jesus' message confirms Swimme's instinct that the enemy must be creatively engaged rather than destroyed. As Haught says, Jesus' "vision was one in which we should allow the weeds to remain along with the wheat . . . The aesthetic urge to harmonize contrasts wins out over the ethical impulse to destroy evil outright."[16] Jesus insisted that God's love was unconditional and universal and that humans must learn to love their enemies in order to further the coming of the Kingdom.

Jesus stands at the reconciling center of all seeming contradiction and paradox. The birth narratives of Luke and Matthew introduce the themes that will form the framework of Jesus' life and message: a fragile, poor, vulnerable, dependent child was yet the strength, the power, royalty, and glory of the great King. Verses from an old English poem, made famous by Benjamin Britten in his *Ceremony of Carols*, capture the delicious paradox of this birth:

> *New Heaven, New War* (Robert Southwell, 1561?–1595)
>
> This little Baby so few days old, is come to rifle Satan's fold;
> All hell doth at his presence quake, though he himself for cold do shake;
> For in this weak unarmèd wise the gates of hell he will surprise.
> With tears he fights and wins the field, his naked breast stands for a
>   shield;
> His battring shot are babish cries, his arrows looks of weeping eyes,
> His martial ensigns cold and need; and feeble flesh his warrior's steed.
> His camp is pitchèd in a stall, his bulwark but a broken wall;
> The crib his trench, haystalks his stakes; of shepherds he his muster
>   makes;
> And thus, as sure his foe to wound, the angels' trumps alarum sound.
> My soul, with Christ join thou in fight; stick to the tents that he hath
>   pight.
> Within his crib is surest ward; this little Babe will be thy guard.
> If thou wilt foil thy foes with joy, then flit not from this heavenly boy.[17]

15. Matt. 13:24–30 (NRSV).

16. Haught, *Cosmic Adventure*, chap. 12, para. 10.

17. Southwell, "New Heaven," sts. 5–8.

Jesus loved life yet was radically open to death; he incarnated complete weakness and true omnipotence; he embraced the heights of joy and the depths of sadness; he was full of God and absorbed the fullness of evil in order to reconcile the two. It is this terrible beauty that attracts the human race, not ultimately his ethical message. He invites his followers to enter deeply into the contradictions of being fully alive. They are invited to love, not hate, their enemies, to embrace death in order to gain life, to lose themselves in order to find themselves. Within the vision of Jesus, it is possible to understand the value of turning the other cheek and pouring heaping coals of kindness upon the enemy's head. The Paschal mystery, the whole journey to life through the path of death, suddenly becomes ultimate common sense, rather than foolish madness.

Jesus' death plumbs the depth of paradox. The Christ who is the sacrament of life descends into annihilation: "No wider or sharper contrast can be imagined than that the infinite embrace the nothingness of death."[18] Who could call the ugliness of the cross beautiful? It is beautiful because the response of Jesus is unreservedly loving. He receives all the squalor of human existence—the hatred, vindictiveness, stupidity, ignorance, and inadequacy of human beings—and transforms it into love, forgiveness, wisdom, knowledge, and maturity. He reveals the radiant beauty that is the potential destiny of the human race. The fullness of human evolution is to become love, and Jesus manifests this possibility on the cross. We are drawn to this beauty and know that our redemption lies there.

Through his manifestation of the beauty of God, Jesus invites humankind to trust in the ultimate goodness of reality. Even though our limited perception of the world causes us to doubt this, Jesus reveals the true beauty of existence. His heroic willingness to embrace the polarities of life in the Universe, reveals the truth of the Kingdom vision: that in the end, love is all in all. Jesus, as the sacrament of God's beauty, is the bridge which connects us to God's dream for the Universe and assures us that what we can grasp "as in a mirror dimly" is true.[19] As Haught points out, this is a vision we sorely need at this time in human history:

> The figure of Jesus as the Christ, as it is portrayed in the Gospels and as it is imitated and re-embodied in contemporary lives, has drawn numerous people into a circle of restored trust and hope. It

18. Haught, *Cosmic Adventure*, chap. 12, para. 11.

19. 1 Cor. 13:12 (NRSV).

has done so, I suspect, because it is a representation of universal beauty in a manner proportionate to a people's experience at this time in the evolution of the Universe. At a time when our primordial trust has been weakened due to our experience of suffering, mortality, guilt and the threat of meaninglessness, an encounter with this picture is capable of allowing us to trust once again that we are cared for and that reality is not indifferent to our deepest longings.[20]

By reconciling all contradiction and paradox within his person, Jesus shows us how to be fully alive. The beauty of his person and message lures us to live in the loving, caring embrace of God who is the one creation journeys from and finds its eternal home in.

20. Haught, *Cosmic Adventure*, chap. 12, para. 6.

BOOK III

The Dream of God

*Then I saw a new heaven and a new earth; for the first heaven and
the first earth had passed away, and the sea was no more. And I
heard a loud voice from the throne saying,*

"See, the home of god is among mortals.

He will dwell with them as their God;

they will be his peoples,

and God himself will be with them;

He will wipe every tear from their eyes.

Death will be no more;

mourning and crying and pain

will be no more,

for the first things have passed away.'

*And the one who was seated on the throne said, 'See, I am making
all things new . . . It is done! I am the Alpha and the Omega, the
beginning and the end.'*[1]

TEILHARD SAYS THAT LOVE is "the fundamental impulse of Life . . .
the one natural medium in which the rising course of evolution can

1. Rev. 21:1, 3–6 (NRSV).

proceed."[2] What does he mean by that? What is this love that gives birth to creation, causes it to evolve, and propels it toward its destiny? I enjoy Brian Swimme's shorthand for Teilhard's philosophy: "The Universe begins with matter, develops into life, develops into thought, develops into God."[3] Religion says that God is love, that love is God, and, therefore, we can say that the Universe is developing into love, but what can we know of this great mystery that is the ocean we swim in, yet is elusive to the grasp of our minds? The great religious texts do their best to describe the nature of love, but how is it manifested in the Universe—in ourselves? This book probes the tip of the iceberg of this subject; it says nothing new but attempts to tell the ancient story one more time in one more way.

The mystery of love reveals a paradox. Like everything else in the Universe, it has two sides—two reciprocal energies that form the balance and the tension necessary to ongoing creativity. The two dialectic forces of love are fullness and emptiness, and they are entirely contingent on one another. Love is a fullness of being that can only be reached through emptiness, loss, and abandonment. This is why mystics from all the religions of the world continually call us to emptiness—because it is the gateway to the bliss of true fulfillment. It is the call to love. This is simply the way the Universe is. It is the pattern that was built into our world right from the beginning, as the infant Universe gradually took on its form through a continual process of death and rebirth. In the very early Universe there were nearly equal amounts of matter and antimatter—a kind of balance between construction and destruction that scientists call thermal equilibrium. As the Universe expanded and cooled, the pairs of particles were annihilated—they canceled each other out. Due to a slight asymmetry favoring matter, everything was not lost, and a small amount of matter survived. It is this matter that constitutes the material of our Universe. And this is only the beginning. The Cosmos lost and found itself countless times as it evolved slowly upward to what we experience today, and it continues on its journey to become an ever more exquisite expression of love. Only utter loss allowed gain and growth. Each time some wonderful aspect of the world came to be, it moved toward annihilation and fell away so that something more beautiful could emerge. Love is an ecstasy of being lost and being found.

2. Teilhard de Chardin, *Future of Mankind*, chap. 3, sec. 4.

3. Bridle, "Divinization of Cosmos."

The next two chapters, which explore the theme of kenosis or self-emptying, continue the theme of suffering. They explore the movement of death, loss, and abandonment so integral to love. Within this vision it is possible to see that all creation has always reflected a kenotic pattern, and that the Christian vision of kenosis is not something new but a continuation and a clarification of the ancient descent/ascent toward love. The cross of Jesus is part of the natural sacrifice of the world. Jesus, the great revealer, shows us the path through death to greater life and points to its deepest significance. He did not create it, but revealed the way to us, giving us hope that it is possible for a human being to become love, thus revealing the possibilities and destiny of humanity. The kenotic journey of Jesus is not the exception to nature's law; it points toward the secret depth hidden in the ancient ways of the Universe. It exemplifies the redeeming pattern of self-sacrifice, loss, and abandonment for the sake of love that is continually on the rise within the evolving Cosmos. The triumph of Jesus' resurrection confirms that death is not the end of life, but a transformative pathway towards fullness and bliss. Nature is not flawed; it did not need to be fixed by a redeeming act that would correct its failings. The pain of loss and abandonment is the groaning of creation on its kenotic journey toward a consummate destiny, a cosmic resurrection.

It is this destiny that will be the subject of the rest of this book. Focused on the sense of promise that the evolving Universe radiates from its very nature, we will probe the future. Can the kenotic pattern of development ever come to a halt? Can the Universe ever reach a fullness where no more sacrifice is necessary? Does love demand an eternal deepening that requires a concomitant eternity of struggle? Can we ever say that we have arrived at what Teilhard calls the Omega Point where love is all in all? What do we mean by heaven? These are the questions to be explored within the theme of promise.

11

Kenosis in the Cosmos—
Becoming Empty to Become Full

There is a great divine "yes" hidden behind and within every "no" of crushing nature. God, who is the line toward rationality and sentience in the upcurrents of the biological pyramid, is also the compassionate lure in, with, and under all purchasing of life at the cost of sacrifice. Long before humans arrived, the way of nature was already a via dolorosa. In that sense, the aura of the cross is cast backward across the whole global story, and it forever outlines the future.[1]

A S A YOUNG PERSON, I was very idealistic and passionate about making a special contribution to the world. No doubt this urgency was born of my upbringing in a devout Catholic world in the days when this was all pervasive. Faith and service were in the water I drank and the air I breathed. In my youthful idealism, I was convinced that life had a clear purpose—heroic self-donation for the good of others. As John F. Kennedy (also from a Catholic background) famously said, "Ask not what your country can do for you, but ask what you can do for your country."[2] A similar zeal inspired my plans for the future. I felt a fiery longing to live a sacrificial life, dedicated to bringing more love into the world. As you would probably guess, at least those of you with Catholic roots, this led me to enter a religious congregation, where I assumed I would find the lifestyle I yearned after. However, as the years went by and I approached the final vows that would seal my commitment, I felt an uneasy apprehension that I was not going to find fulfillment in religious life. An emptiness or hollowness seemed to reside somewhere in my innards. Certain thoughts pricked my mind and awakened a profound questioning within.

1. Rolston, "Kenosis in Nature," 59–60.
2. Kennedy, *Inaugral Address.*

I remembered a good friend telling me with great conviction that she intended to marry because she believed that it was God's usual way of teaching people how to love. In marriage, she told me, there is an inbuilt system for altruism. Every day you get up and there are your spouse and children needing every ounce of love and care that you possess. You do not have to look any further to give yourself away. Without family life you have to work hard at not becoming selfish. Marriage, she told me, if lived correctly, is a great way to make a difference in the world, person by person. Recently, I found this excerpt from *Beauty* by John O'Donohue that captures what she was saying perfectly: "In psychological and spiritual circles people talk of overcoming the ego. Being a loving parent is work that guarantees the transformation of the ego for in the work of rearing children the limits of your selfishness, need and smallness are continually challenged. Somehow you find within your heart a love that is willing to stretch further and further."[3]

As I pondered these things I realized that in religious life it was necessary to begin each new day by choosing to love, a kind of daily recommitment to service, and I did not think I was up to it. As you have no doubt guessed by now, I met a partner with whom I felt deeply at home, with whom I could build a loving marriage, and I left religious life.

This plunge into the chaotic world of marriage and parenthood was fearful for me, because I knew that it would demand everything I had and was. I drew courage from Kahlil Gibran's famous poem on the nature of love, which manifested both the comforts and demands of real love. I hoped that I could follow the rigorous path of love so that I would not only plumb the depths of my own heart, but also become a part of the heart of the Universe. In the twenty-one years that have now passed, I have tasted the heights and depths, the laughter and the tears of family life.[4] Marriage and parenthood have proven to be the hardest and best things I have ever known.

I believe that the truest vocation for all human beings lies in finding the most excellent way that they can achieve kenosis, or more simply, the best way that they can give themselves away and in so doing, find themselves. The Universe models this and requires it for the realization of its own destiny—to become love. Despite its grand theme, kenosis, or the

3. O'Donahue, *Beauty*, 164.

4. Gibran, *The Prophet*, 12.

gift of self, happens day by day in all the small and major decisions we are faced with. Kenosis is a great mystery, the ultimate paradox of life, and the only path towards wholeness and fulfillment. It draws us into the heart of God—the heart of nature, which is kenotic in its very essence. The one who enters its burning embrace must lose everything in order to gain everything. Jesus, the great teacher, taught us that those who are prepared to lose their lives will ultimately find them,[5] and he demonstrated this truth with the gift of himself.

KENOSIS AND THE NATURE OF THE COSMOS

The word *kenosis,* a Greek word referring to the action of self-emptying, is traditionally associated in Christian circles with Christ's self-emptying in his life, death and resurrection.[6] In this chapter the term will be used more broadly to include the sacrificial elements that are an integral part of the Cosmos, and indeed a necessary part of each human being's life. In an attempt at a creative synthesis, we will look at some of the ways theology and science have contributed to this concept. Although the movement toward emptiness is a central theme in all the religious traditions, as usual, we will simply focus on Christian insights.

Life as it is in this constantly changing and evolving world is kenotic by nature. The continual ebb and flow of losing and finding is as close to us as our breathing in and out. Brian Swimme sees this pattern reflected in every facet of reality. In *The Hidden Heart of the Cosmos*, Swimme speaks passionately about the need for a new myth to help humans grasp the significance of the continuing kenosis of the Universe and enable them to enter more fully into the mystery of loss, death, and rebirth. He suggests that if we stop looking at the creations of the Universe as dead objects, we would be drawn into the creative dynamics all around us. As an example, he points to the Sun of the Milky Way solar system. Four million tons of hydrogen are required every second by the Sun in order that it continue to sustain the life of all the creatures of the Earth. That same hydrogen existed for millions of years before being suddenly used up for the sake of the Sun's continued existence and the life of the Earth. The planet's creatures have evolved to be able to capture energy from the Sun and transform it into life. Human beings are part of the food chain

5. Matt. 10:39 (NRSV).

6. Phil. 2:5–11 (NRSV).

that consumes the Sun's energy in many forms. Swimme tell us that "for four million years, humans have been feasting on the Sun's energy stored in the form of wheat or maize or reindeer as each day the Sun dies as Sun and is reborn as the vitality of the Earth."[7] To contemplate the energy requirement of life is itself a revelation—a shattering as Swimme calls it. He urges us to think of all the life forms and elements of the Universe that were necessary to give us this moment. Everything has been given to us and everything is required of us as it has been for all entities within creation since the first moment. To embrace loss is to be part of the flow of existence. Within the interconnectedness of the Universe, current life forms only exist because of the sacrifice of all that went before and the continuing sacrifice pervasive in nature. Kenotic, self-sacrificing love, is fundamental to life in the Universe.

KENOSIS GIVES BIRTH TO NEWNESS

The sacrificial mode of being is the source of novelty in the Universe, bringing new surprising things to life that could never have been anticipated. For instance, Swimme speaks of the supernova explosion of the star Tiamat, which gave birth to our own solar system, as a sacrifice that enabled entirely new substances to be formed, substances vital to the ongoing development of life in the Universe:

> Out of the spectacular tensions in the stellar core, Tiamat had forged tungsten, copper, and vanadium. She vanished as a star in her grand finale of beauty, but the essence of her creativity went forth in wave after wave of fluorine, astatine, and bromine. Tossed into the night sky with the most extravagant gesture of generosity were cesium, silver, and silicon. Tiamat had evoked magnesium, osmium, gallium, rhodium, and titanium—each a new world of power cast forth by the quintillions for the future unfolding of the Universe . . . None of these power elements had appeared in the primeval fireball or in the early galactic era.[8]

The death of one thing leads to the emergence of new forms. The very fact of death was invented by the Universe as an essential ingredient of growth and expansion. The earliest form of life scientists have been able to find, the prokaryote, did not have natural death built into its sys-

7. Swimme, *Hidden Heart*, 41–42.

8. Berry and Swimme, *Universe Story*, 61.

tem. It did not die unless something killed it; in fact it is possible that there are prokaryotes alive today that are four billion years old. Therefore, for the first two billion years of life on Earth, death was not inevitable.[9] The prokaryotes, which were the primal cells, did not reproduce through sexuality, and therefore, they did not become too numerous for the planet to sustain. However, in order to produce more novelty and diversity, the Universe invented meiotic sex (basic genetic exchange) within the eukaryote cells, which were the descendents of the prokaryotes, and an immense flowering in the life forms of the Earth was initiated. However, with the emergence of sexuality, death became a necessity so that the planet would not become overwhelmed with members of new species and so that more novelty could be achieved.

EMBRACING LOSS

Death and loss then are fundamental aspects of creativity. I remember how shocked and upset I was when I first heard Brian Swimme speak about suffering and loss. I was listening to his *Canticle to the Cosmos* series on audiotape, and I have a vivid memory of his voice shouting ecstatically, "Everything, everything will be lost. Absolutely everything will vanish. The Universe is one great flashing show. Everything will be consumed and return to mystery. Nothing will remain."[10] He sounded as if he thought this was a great thing, but I found myself wondering about the horrendous waste of it all. What could possibly be the point of all this beauty and all this suffering if it was going to simply vanish, being consumed by some ravenous vacuum like a giant black hole? How could all this loss be such a good thing? Then I remembered also hearing from Swimme that the Universe never lost anything of value, and it reminded me of a holy card that I used to carry around with me. I can't recall the exact wording of it, but it went something like, "Nothing is ever finally lost, and all in the end is harvest." Then I understood what Swimme was trying to get across. He was saying that we must accept the fundamental fact that every single thing in the Universe and in our own lives is going to disappear, that we cannot hold on to anything, that there is no permanence in this world. And once we have made this leap, we can come to understand that everything of any value at all will be found in a new way

9. Swimme, *Universe is Green Dragon*, 113.

10. Swimme, *Canticle to Cosmos*, 5.

by the Universe, or in religious terms, by God. Every effort we have ever made to love selflessly, every tiny good deed we have ever done, every gorgeous blossoming of spring flowers, every wag of a dog's tail is taken and transformed into more love, more life, more beauty. This is what fuels evolution practically and spiritually. All is lost so that it can be found again as the world spirals upward toward the fullness of God.

When it comes to human beings, the natural kenotic patterns of nature take on an additional refinement because now kenosis is not simply instinctive as it is in all other creatures and life forms, but now it can be freely chosen, or rejected, as the case may be. To the extent that humans are simply an interconnected part of nature, they are subject to the same laws of birth and death as every other entity on Earth. However, on the other hand, it is possible to say that we humans are the only inhabitants of the planet that could be described as truly capable of kenosis in its fullest meaning. Philosopher Holmes Rolston III makes this point in his contribution to a collection of writings on cosmic kenosis called *The Work of Love: Creation as Kenosis*. He asserts that only human beings are moral agents within nature; only they can freely choose self-transcendence for the sake of another.[11] Other living entities are bound by instinct and genetic coding and cannot be altruistic; neither can they be selfish. Perhaps this distinction is too anthropocentric though. It seems to me that we draw the line too firmly between ourselves and other species on the planet. Stories abound of dogs and other pets that appear to put loyalty and love above their own survival needs, even sacrificing themselves to protect their human owners. The simplicity of their devotion is very moving. I would say that humans, in their freedom and developed self-reflective consciousness, are capable of manifesting the deepest, most explicit expressions of kenotic love among Earth's creatures, but other animals certainly seem to be loving and giving in ways that are surprising and inspirational.

In any case, Rolston is far from thinking there is no kenosis in nature apart from humankind. He acknowledges that the human ability for kenotic expression is simply the flowering of a seed planted at the outset of life's emergence. Love has been on the rise within nature since the beginning, probing for higher levels of expression. Kenosis has always been present in nature and will continue to emerge in ever more explicit terms.

11. Rolston, "Kenosis and Nature," 43.

He puts it this way: "Biological nature is always giving birth, regenerating, always in travail. Something is always dying and something is always living on . . . Perhaps we can begin to recognize in creative nature, dimensions both of redemptive and of vicarious suffering, one whereby ongoing success is achieved by sacrifice."[12] Rolston sees divine purpose shining through the whole. All living things do their part in the ongoing creation of the Universe and in this they "share the labor of divinity."[13]

THE SUMPTUOUS FEAST

The generosity of the Universe calls forth and demands a generous response in human beings. Loss is going to happen to us whether we embrace it or we dig in our heels and are dragged kicking and screaming into the future. Swimme suggests that it would be better if we join what he calls the feast of giving, the giving over of our best selves for the continuing creativity of the Universe and the growth of love. Simply put, we need to find our own particular ways of giving ourselves away so that we may reach our own fulfillment and participate in divine creativity.

There is always an interesting tension between selfishness and selflessness woven into the fabric of life. Is giving yourself away so that you may find yourself a selfish or selfless orientation? Certain followers of Darwin suggest that there is no such thing as real altruism either in nature or in human beings. They argue that all life forms act selfishly for the sake of preservation and propagation. The most famous of these in recent times is Richard Dawkins. In his controversial book *The Selfish Gene*, he paints a picture of nature's basic functions as being inherently selfish, not in the sense that flies or fish have motives for acting, but in the sense that at the genetic level, survival is the only thing that genes are wired for. It is impossible to speak of this subject without the use of metaphor. Dawkins contends that genes simply want to replicate themselves and live on in as robust a fashion as possible. Therefore, the survival of the fittest is their only operating mode. From the selfish gene's point of view, the organism that hosts it is only there to meet its needs, that is, to provide resources so that it can copy itself. To the extent that the host is healthy, the genes are content because they can continue to flourish. However, the destruction of this host is eventually necessary to create room for offspring that

12. Ibid., 58.
13. Ibid., 59.

continue the life of the genes. The argument is then that genes are entirely selfish. Dawkins' book also suggests that human cultural evolution has proceeded according to this same selfish premise.

Obviously, there is some truth in what Dawkins says, but are the ideas he presents the whole truth? I suggest that this is only half the story of nature's pattern of evolution. Rolston has written a book called *Genes, Genesis and God* in which he offers a rebuttal of Dawkins' contention. He argues that life operates just as much on the principles of cooperation and caring as it does on selfishness and aggression, and that the survival of the sharers works better as a description of life's continuance than the survival of the fittest. He ridicules the notion that altruism does not exist in human society by referring to the Good Samaritan of biblical fame in satirical terms as only helping the wounded stranger on the road to Jericho in order to strengthen his genetic line. He concludes, "What a hypocrite! That selfish bastard!"[14]

As we have seen in book 1, Lynn Margulis has done innovative work on symbiosis to show that the Universe does not thrive on competition, but rather on the principle of altruism. Her work reveals that cooperation and sacrifice are more fundamental to evolution than competition and the survival of the fittest. She speaks of new species arising from the merging of organisms into a symbiotic union, sacrificing independent existence for the sake of creating new beings. She suggests that this cooperation and willingness to sacrifice for the sake of the future are more compelling than the argument for competitive natural selection.[15]

In nature, everything must live off something else. There is no such thing as rugged individualism, and pure selfishness gets us nowhere. One could argue against Dawkins that it is self-centeredness rather than altruism that is actually impossible to achieve within the web of existence. In human society it appears that trampling on the needs of the others and taking care of number one is successful in terms of what could be considered the optimum in living: fame, fortune, and power. However, as all sacred texts point out, the wicked do not really prosper; in fact, as human beings, they shrink and sometimes disappear. The Universe can only use what is of value for building the kingdom of love; therefore, selfish acts cannot be harvested. What about selfish people? Perhaps they become

14. Rolston, *Genes, Genesis and God*, 253.

15. Margulis, *Symbiotic Planet*.

so tiny in terms of their humanity that they cannot make it through to the fullness of life. Theologically, one might say that a definition of hell is non-existence due to a lifetime of selfish choices. Or maybe shrunken people pass through death as shadows that can be revived and built up through exposure to love. Theologically, this could be a definition of purgatory. If the reader is fascinated by these ideas, I suggest the book *The Great Divorce*, by C. S. Lewis. At the end of this book we will delve into this a little.

An excruciating paradox lies at the heart of our discussion of kenosis. Personally, I can get in touch with this by pondering my position as a consumer within my habitat. By consumer I mean one who must have a constant supply of energy to continue existing. When I stop and think about my energy requirements, I have a sense of horror at what I am forced to do. I must destroy the lives of animals and plants to build up my body; continually take in oxygen which was created by my bacterial forebears to keep the flow of life going within me; take in water, a precious resource, to hydrate my thirsty frame; and absorb light and energy from the Sun to ensure my growth and strength. I know that energy is not limitless and that it could run out for me at any time as it has for countless life forms all over the planet. I am grateful that I do not have to beg for food or survive drought and famine as millions of people do. I feel very selfish—that I am a taker at the top of the food chain.

Yet, is it wrong for me to thrive? What I am trying to get at here is there is a need for all living beings to receive the sacrifice of others, to be selfish in a sense. All life forms on Earth have to share in a limited source of energy. To the degree that this is a balanced, equitable sharing, the Earth community as a whole can thrive, but if this becomes unbalanced, in the sense that some claim more than their share, then great destruction inevitably follows. The aboriginal peoples of the Americas managed to keep this energy balance for thousands of years, living an entirely sustainable lifestyle, sharing energy with other natural life forms. They saw themselves as part of the system. 'Civilized' people have managed to degrade the land in a devastating way in the last few hundred years, putting the whole equilibrium of the continent off kilter. We have been takers not sharers.

David Suzuki, in the fascinating book he wrote with Peter Knudtson, *Wisdom of the Elders,* shares the ecological insight of some of these First Nations. According to the Desana people of the northwestern Amazon, it is paramount for us to recognize that life on Earth all draws from a finite reservoir of energy, and any species that consumes more than its proper portion makes it unavailable for use by other creatures. This knowledge "imposes upon humans a conscious obligation to limit their energy use so that other forms of life will be assured of their rightful share of nature's rigid budget of energy."[16]

Nature is full of sacrifice, and the system works well as long as everyone gets involved in what Swimme calls the feast of giving. This is how Suzuki and Knudtson put it:

> Ecology also has much to say, albeit indirectly, about the notion of 'sacrifice' in nature. By means of feedback loops a mature tree in a tropical forest ecosystem can help perpetuate its own kind, as well as its fellow species, by gradually relinquishing its energy-and-mineral-laden leaves. These leaves enrich the meager forest-floor soils so that new seedlings can grow. Another tree within the same forest, routinely 'sacrifices' a portion of its fruit bounty to clown-beaked toucan; the turtle, a portion of its leathery eggs to marauding rodent; the tapir, its war, blood-infused flesh to the poison-tipped darts of an Amazonian hunter's blowgun. The hunter, as well as his kin, will eventually yield to the same stern unspoken ethos of ecological sacrifice, however reluctantly, when his body becomes a feast for teeming populations of various decomposing organisms.[17]

Giving and taking in balanced measure is absolutely essential to life, but the demand that this makes upon human beings is that we see ourselves as an integral part of nature, and therefore, we live each day with gratitude that nourishment in its many forms is still available as a costly gift.

There is a powerful and ultimately healthy urgency within each one of us to thrive, to reach the heights of our own possibilities. According to Swimme, the task of each human being is to become the unique person nature intended in its gift of abundant differentiation. No one else, past, present, or to come, is exactly like me, and it is my duty to develop the potential of my distinct personhood as much as possible—to stand up and say who I am. This striving upward for personal fulfillment is healthy and good. A tiny baby forms in its mother's womb and begins the journey to

16. Knudtson and Suzuki, *Wisdom of Elders*, 169.
17. Ibid., 160.

maturity by following a purely egocentric path. A growing child necessarily takes what it needs from its family and environment and surges forth to seize life. Slowly, imperceptibly, the tide changes as this child reaches maturity and life begins to demand reciprocity, self-donation, and sacrifice. The fully-grown person fits into the world through considering others, sharing life with a partner, learning to sacrifice personal needs for the sake of offspring and the demands of providing sustenance to others. Another deep need gradually makes itself felt: the need to give the self away. Our selfishness gives way to selflessness as we learn life's lessons of letting go—of our children, our good looks, our bodily strength, and ultimately our life. If we embrace this natural movement, we learn the power of kenosis in our lives. We discover the treasures that lie hidden in the depths of self if we let go of ego needs. We come to understand that the path to fullness lies on the other side of emptiness and loss. Selfishness and selflessness are deeply intertwined in yet another yin-yang reality at the heart of life. They are the movement into love.

12

Kenosis and the Nature of God

I AM FASCINATED BY discussions on the nature of God. It is an inexhaustible subject and has been explored by human beings since they came down from the trees and started to ponder where they came from. The history of religion reflects the multitude of images and ideas that have come to people over time within the variety of human cultures. Does God reveal the divine nature to us, or do we have to figure it out ourselves? Perhaps it is a combination of the two. The sacred scriptures of the world's religions record the deepest intimations within the human soul about who God is. Divine epiphanies, such as inexplicable burning bushes, have invited people to move beyond their rational capabilities and plunge into the heart of mysterious presence. I believe there is a space where divine revelation and human understanding meet, and out of this flow our ideas about God. All of these, every last one of them, is a metaphor, a holy card that helps us draw close to mystery, but must ultimately be discarded in the face of the unspeakable and inexpressible reality of God. The theological ideas that I would like to discuss for a while must be seen in this light. Hopefully, they will serve their purpose and help us along our journey.

Earlier on we visited the idea that the Universe erupted from a fertile emptiness or all-nourishing abyss. Brian Swimme probes the nature of this womb of all being. He speaks of the source of the Universe as ultimate mystery, but he also identifies one of its chief characteristics as ultimate generosity: "Emptiness is permeated with the urgency to leap forth . . . the ground of being is *generosity*. The ultimate source of all that is, the support and well of being, is Ultimate Generosity. All being comes forth and shines, glimmers and glistens, because the root reality of the Universe is generosity of being. That's *why* the ground of being is empty: every *thing* has been given over to the Universe; all existence has been poured forth; all Generosity retains no thing."[1]

Swimme does not use the word *God*, but I would like to. I want to say that God, who is the source of everything, pours out creation from the divine being in an act of kenotic love. Creation is God's self-donation. Christian theologian Jürgen Moltmann has developed a theology of creation along these lines. It reflects the traditional Judeo-Christian belief that God and the Universe are separate, and not one and the same thing as a monistic religion such as Buddhism would suggest. I present Moltmann's thoughts in a spirit of openness with no dogmatic intent. They are interesting ideas.

ZIMZUM

Moltmann's understanding of kenosis is rooted in the Jewish kabbalistic teaching of *zimzum*. This creation myth starts with the God of fullness and infinity—God is the totality of all that is. If God is unlimited and eternal, there is no space for anything else, no room for creation. So the story goes that "[i]n the free overflowing rapture of his love, the eternal God goes out of himself and makes a creation."[2] *Zimzum* submits that God chose to contract the divine presence to produce the space for creation to exist. Therefore, God chose to withdraw in order to make room for the world. After the contraction, a void of non-being came into existence because anything outside the source of all being must be non-being. However, some traces of the divine were left behind and became the material substance for creation. Therefore, God created the world outside Godself.

One of the key questions that immediately arises from this assertion is why God would choose to create the world in this manner. Moltmann gives a twofold answer. The first one is connected to freedom: God wanted creation to exist freely and therefore, had to create the space within which true choice and freedom was a possibility. God lovingly withdrew God's complete presence so that creation was not overwhelmed by the creator and could be separate and free.[3] The second reason is that a void was necessary in order for God to create. If there were no space beyond God, nothing new could come to be because God is utter completeness.

1. Swimme, *Universe is Green Dragon*, 146.

2. Moltmann, *God in Creation*, 15.

3. Ibid., 91.

Moltmann says, "It is only a withdrawal by God into himself that can free the space into which God can act creatively."[4] God is not absent from the world. The divine presence pervades everything, and indeed the Universe emerges from divine seed. However, in order to respect the freedom of this budding offspring, it is a veiled presence, which lovingly chooses not to overwhelm creation, leaving some distance and choice.

There are several movements in Moltmann's understanding of creation. The first is the most dramatic. In order to create, God chooses to humble the divine self. Kenosis begins before creation emerges. God withdraws his being, which is the source of what mystics have called is-ness, creating nothingness, literally God-forsaken space. Given the fact that Christian theology defines hell as the absolute loss of God—non-life, non-existence, non-love—then this space literally becomes hell: "The *nihil* in which God creates his creation is God-forsakenness, hell, absolute death; and it is against the threat of this that he maintains his creation in life."[5] Divine creativeness is a continual ongoing process as God faithfully sustains and nurtures the world in its journey of growth and development from the cosmic egg. As theologians tell us, if God forgot about us for a moment, the whole enterprise would disappear.

The second movement introduces God's plan to help the world along toward its destiny, which is to come home to the fullness of God. From the beginning, God resolved to be present in the world to save it from hell. The Christ figure now enters the scene as the savior who sacramentalizes the life-saving, life-giving power of God. Through Christ, God "pervades the space of God-forsakenness with his presence," overcoming nothingness with God's glory.[6] Through the cosmic Christ figure, who is seen to have eternally existed and is made visible in time through the person of Jesus of Nazareth, the kenotic dimension of God suffering with and for creation is made explicit. The humility of God in limiting and withdrawing his presence in order to create the world is continued in the kenosis of Jesus, who pours out God's love as lifeblood, emptying himself to pervade the void with a lifesaving transfusion. This did not happen at a particular moment in time. The movement of outpouring love that began at the first moment of creation is made explicit in the cross of Jesus. Thus,

4. Ibid., 86.

5. Ibid., 87–88.

6. Ibid., 91.

the new creation emerges from "the history of God's suffering."[7] The hell of nothingness is pervaded by the heaven of fullness.

Therefore, the third movement of creation is an eschatological one. At the end of the journey, the world comes of age by being transformed into the kingdom of love, where God is once again all in all and all traces of hell have been overcome. The act of creation itself contained the seeds of this all-consuming redemption, which is symbolized by Christ's resurrection. Jesus' triumph over death is a finger pointing to the ultimate direction of the world's journey, and the promise of this all-consuming glory is already present at the dawn of creation: "So the resurrection and the kingdom of glory are the fulfillment of the promise which creation itself represents."[8]

Theologian Keith Ward has developed a useful shorthand model of Moltmann's three movements: kenosis, enosis, and theosis. *Kenosis* occurs at the beginning of creation—God's self-emptying to allow a truly free creation to emerge. *Enosis* is the second and interim stage of the process, whereby God reaches out to creation through Jesus, drawing it into a partial unity, a mutual indwelling that transforms created beings into the likeness of God. The final, eschatological, stage of the cosmic process, Ward calls *theosis*, where God becomes all in all: "The Cosmos will be fully integrated into the life of God . . . In the moment of theosis, the Cosmos is transfigured to become the unrestricted manifestation of God's glory."[9] The only function of kenosis is to make possible theosis.

LIFE IN THE VOID

I find this creation myth very compelling for several reasons. To begin with, it gives an explanation of why hell, suffering, and evil exist in the first place. Hell was not caused by some devil or disobedience on the part of creatures, it is simply a necessary correlative to existence. If the Universe is to exist at all, then hell must also exist. This argument confirms the idea that hell is not a place of torture that humans are sent to because of wrongdoing, it is non-reality, non-existence, non-love. It is the absence of God. It is necessary because the world is free.

7. Ibid., 90.
8. Ibid., 90.
9. Ward, "Cosmos and Kenosis," 166.

Another reason I like this story is because it describes the nature of God as completely loving, compassionate, and giving. It protects the complete goodness of God. There is an answer to the question of how non-reality, non-love, suffering, and death could exist when God, from whom everything comes, is the fullness of life and love. There is no dark side to God from which evil comes and no need for a devil. Within this framework, God remains perfect in love and being, and hell exists only as a contraction of that nature so that creation can exist at all. I like Moltmann's myth because it complements what I have been trying to say about suffering and death—that it is a necessary part of the journey toward the fullness of love. It fits well with the story of evolution told by science and developed by spiritual geniuses such as Teilhard into a cosmology. It also explains why human beings have a deep-rooted sense of cosmic homelessness, of not feeling fully at home within the Universe—that their final destiny has not been reached yet. Perhaps this tremendous desire for completion, happiness and home, arises in humans from the unconscious awareness that they live partially in hell, and they long to experience heaven, the fullness of existence. This hell is pervaded by heaven because God is always present in all aspects of creation, but it is a veiled presence and human beings still feel their separateness from God as a terrible suffering.

Jesus comes into our world to show us the way home—in other words, to save us from hell. The deepest meaning of the kenosis of Jesus is that he suffers hell with us. He lives in the void with us, experiencing the painful veil between God and creation, pouring himself out to bring more love into the world. Jesus shows us the way home to oneness with God—with love and life itself. The journey of life is each person's opportunity to become a part of God. We are created in the kenotic vacuum and live suspended between heaven and hell, sustained only by the loving yet oblique presence of God, while we learn to choose true existence, while we learn to choose heaven. If we decide to live in selfishness and egotism, we move ourselves in the wrong direction, the ultimate terminus of which is permanent death—non-love. If we respond to the lure of love, we are on the road to becoming eternally one with God's being. This is not simply the path of individuals, but the road toward fulfillment of the whole Cosmos. As Teilhard says, the Universe is evolving toward love and unity, lured by God, but this is not automatic because creation is free. The choices we make in how we live either hasten the journey or move the world backwards.

The nature of divinity is love poured out. God is not a coercer, but a lover who practices self-restraint, waiting and hoping for an ever-deepening response of love from creation. Therefore, God is vulnerable to us in desiring to be loved in return. This is the nature of love—it woos us gently, generously and patiently, inviting not forcing a response.

JESUS, THE KENOSIS OF GOD

Many theologians, over the centuries, have fought philosophical battles over whether God is impervious to the goings on in our world, or whether God suffers with creation within the paradox of existence. Theological responses have ranged from God as the unmoved mover of classical scholasticism to the fellow traveler who understands of process theology. Moltmann comes down somewhere in the middle of this debate, insisting that God is utterly vulnerable to creation, but by divine will and choice rather than necessity. For him, God truly suffers with creation. In his most famous book, *The Crucified God,* he says that it was not a lonely Jesus on the cross paying back humanity's debt to the Father, but the whole Trinity was there, suffering to redeem the world. In the *zimzum* myth, Moltmann again points to the empathic, compassionate God who is willing to allow hell to exist, the godless void created by divine contraction, in order to share the glories of his being and give creation the possibility of becoming part of God. Jesus manifests God's willingness to become immersed in hell for creation's sake. This is the gift of the Christ figure, which draws the human heart and mind into an unfathomable mystery. God enters the antithesis of God in order to lure and cajole creation to its destiny.

The incarnation, death, and resurrection of Jesus shine a path of light within this dark mystery and allow us to glimpse the heart of kenosis. I want to take the story of Jesus out of the fall/redemption model, which is based on the fall of creation from a perfect state due to the disobedience of human creatures. According to this myth, which still predominates in Christian doctrine, Jesus' incarnation and death were a necessary sacrifice to repair this damage done by humans and bring creation back into a right relationship with the Creator. The Christian Eucharist celebrates this victory. From my point of view, it is indeed a sacrifice that we celebrate in the Eucharist, but not the kind of sacrifice that appeases God or that pays the price for human disobedience. It is the kenosis of the creator God that we celebrate in Jesus. His death continues the outpouring that has always been present in creation from its beginning and reveals the depths of divine love that is willing to suffer all the pains of hell in order to lead the way to the fullness of heaven. Jesus' death is the sacrament of the kenosis of God. It teaches us that we too (the Universe too) must choose the divine path of self-sacrificing love and suffer through to joy and unending life.

The Eucharist is the thanksgiving celebration of Jesus' passage through suffering and hell to joy and fulfillment. His resurrection is the answer to his kenosis on the cross. He models for creation the transformation possible when suffering and death are embraced for the cause of love and new life. Jesus exemplifies the path of redemptive suffering that has always been present in the Universe and reveals the way through the darkness to the light.

Theologian John Haught sees the reason for all kenosis in the resurrection of Christ. All acts of self-emptying, kenotic suffering cannot be ends in themselves because the overwhelming direction of life is towards greater existence gained through sacrifice. The resurrection gives witness to the boundless possibilities for unlimited life that rise from the ashes of self-transcendence. In his cross and resurrection Jesus reveals the true nature of the God of life: "But if Jesus is the sacrament of God's own reality, as Christian faith teaches, we must conclude once again that the essential content of revelation is nothing other than the *kenosis* of God that opens up the future to an all-inclusive vision promised in the resurrection. What finally becomes manifest in Jesus, and especially in his death, is that the promising mystery that embraces our world is, at heart, utterly self-emptying love."[10]

Seeking to be faithful to the way of Jesus, Christianity urges humanity to be poured out for others, to strive for justice, to suffer for the sake of the happiness and fulfillment of the world. Jesus used the symbol of the feast to illustrate his message and show us how to become food for one another: "Take, eat; this is my body . . . this is my blood of the covenant, which is poured out."[11] At the time of Jesus, in the Jewish mindset there was no sense of a division of body and soul within persons. The body

10. Haught, *Mystery and Promise*, chap. 6, para. 47.

11. Matt. 26:27–28 (NRSV).

referred to the whole being and blood meant life. Jesus was saying in effect, "Take my life and my whole self as nourishment for your greater life and do the same for each other." This is the feast of giving that Jesus speaks of, modeling it with his own life and death. This is the kenosis of the Universe made manifest.

13

Becoming Full of God

Time is not the fullness of being. There is existence and there is emp-
tiness. Both are real. The eternal, the transphenomenal, shows itself
in time, yes, just as the dynamics of the Cosmos show themselves in
concrete events. But what is invisible is real as well.[1]

I pray that you may have the power to comprehend, with all the
saints, what is the breadth and length and height and depth, and to
know the love of Christ that surpasses knowledge, so that you may
be filled with all the fullness of God. Now to [God] who by the power
at work within us is able to accomplish abundantly far more than all
we can ask or imagine, to [God] be glory in the church and in Christ
Jesus to all generations, forever and ever. Amen.[2]

WHERE ARE WE GOING? Where is this astonishing, arduous journey
taking us? It is quite foolish to speculate about the ultimate destiny of the Cosmos from within our tiny, human brains, yet the desire to
know the end of the story is insurmountable. We want to know where
we are going. It is difficult for our present lives to have meaning without
this because "Where are we going?" is a very close relative of "What is
the purpose of our lives?" I have to confess that I have been obsessed
with these questions since childhood. Growing up within Christianity,
I felt a certain comfort and security within the traditional response to
end things—at least in terms of the end of an individual's life. I had, and
still have, a strong belief that all people who do their best to live in love
will find themselves in the embrace of God on the other side of death.
However, over the years I became completely agnostic about the end of
the world, not being able to make much of a second coming of Christ

1. Swimme, *Hidden Heart*, 97.
2. Eph. 3:18–21 (NRSV).

along with apocalyptic disaster. I had a sense of purpose regarding what my life was about, but when it came to the world, I felt mostly misery and bewilderment at the seeming uselessness of the ways of the Universe. My faith gave me a vision of the human journey of life and death passing into eternity, but it did not really address the vast evolutionary journey of the Cosmos. Looking up into the stars at night as a child, I couldn't imagine how my Jesus could be the savior of all that. The story of people seemed too insignificant to matter very much, and I wondered if my God was just one small god in the Universe.

MATTERS OF DESTINY

When we ponder the future within an eco-spiritual perspective, we are concerned with not only the destiny of individual people, or even humanity as a whole, but also our planet Earth and ultimately the whole Cosmos. We can see the Earthly life of each creature coming to an end, but we have yet to comprehend the fate of our planet (although we worry about it all the time), and the end of the world is so far ahead that we can only guess the outcome. Yet, I think we need to consider the whole picture as one movement—one destiny. I want to explore an overarching cosmology that gives meaning and purpose to the journey of each particle of existence and to the entire show in space-time and beyond.

Speaking of time, it is really rather strange that we assume that there will be a future. Any speculation about the ultimate destiny of the world needs to be seen against the backdrop of the great mystery of Time. Annie Dillard tells us, "We live and move by splitting the light of the present, as a canoe's bow parts water . . . We open time as a boat's stem slits the crest of the present."[3] To think of the future, even the next moment, plunges us into the terrifying and wondrous mystery of contingency. Imagine all that exists right now—the whole swirling Cosmos down to your own tiny being—and then imagine all the billions of years that make up the past— and now know that none of it will exist one split second into the future. If we were able to stop all our present moments slipping into the past, stop time for a little while, we would be standing at the edge of a great abyss, or a great wall. Creation occurs second by second. It is a miracle that what is now continues on. What does the future unfold into? What is this ocean of existence or non-existence that the bow of our canoe opens?

3. Dillard, *For the Time Being*, 186, 203.

The Universe has been expanding since it flared out of eternity. We want to ask, "What is it expanding into?" The scientists tell us that this is the wrong question, that the Cosmos creates time and space as it goes. The future knocks us to our knees, and our minds acquiesce to mystery.

Having said that, I should now put down my metaphorical pen and stop probing matters I cannot hope to understand with my tiny pinprick of consciousness. But of course I cannot. I need at least a hint of what it is that is opening up before us. I am spurred on by a sense of promise that the evolving Universe radiates from its very nature. The suffering and kenosis we have dwelt on so much must have an answer. Can the rough seas of present existence ever dissolve into a peaceful swell without destroying the very nature of beauty? Is there ever going to be a resurrection that requires no more crucifixions? Is there a heaven, and what could it be if there is?

We have been describing kenosis as just one side of the coin, as being necessary only for the sake of theosis as Keith Ward describes it—being full of the utter fullness of God. The remaining chapters of this book are about becoming full, about the realization in time and eternity of God's promises to the Cosmos.

Religion has always played a vital part in conceptualizing the hope the human race has in achieving everlasting life. The task of religion is to make the leap beyond what we can know and experience, but this leap must be vitally connected with the material, spiritual Universe. The problem in the past was there was no continuity within theology about this world and a possible next. Heaven was conceived as a place completely separate and other than this Universe. I agree with theologians John Polkinghorne and Michael Welker that any probing of the future destiny of the world must be situated within both continuity and discontinuity.[4] What eternity will be like is both a continuation of what we know now and a discontinuation that allows for the resolution of present tensions. Heaven will in some way be a natural evolution of present existence and yet surpass it in ways that our imagination is too limited to grasp. As we shall see, following a belief in continuity alone leaves us forever bound within the laws of the Universe, never achieving our final destiny. Embracing discontinuity as well means that the world's evolving is a journey with a specific destination—the utter fullness of love.

---

4. Polkinghorne and Welker, *End of World*, 4.

I do not pretend that there are any final answers within the realm of eschatology. A healthy agnosticism is surely an absolute requirement for peering into the far future and speculating about the ultimate destiny of the world. It is in that spirit that I tentatively probe the possibilities that arise from what we know about the nature of reality and what the longings of the human heart can tell us. Three scenarios present themselves for examination: the first is that there is no afterlife beyond this world, and the destiny of the Cosmos is simply to be, to exist; the second is that there is some type of realm which continues after death, but it operates within basically the same laws as this world with continual change necessitating continued struggle into eternity; the third is that there is a realm beyond death which is an evolution of the current state of the Universe, where continuity is maintained but also a radical discontinuity is inaugurated which resolves present polarities. As we look at these possibilities we should not forget they are just that. Imagination plays a creative role in this regard; in fact, it may be the most suitable power to employ as we try to enter the dream of the Earth as Thomas Berry calls it, or more suitably for this study, the dream of God.

REALITY IS STORY SHAPED

I believe that the epic of the Universe is a story with a beginning, middle, and end. The shape of human storytelling continues to fascinate me. We have already reflected on the role of conflict within literature, how we need the antagonist to bring out the best in the hero. Now I want to delve into what happens at the end of a tale—the falling action and resolution—because I believe that stories reveal not only our deepest longings for fulfillment, but also our strongest intuitions of our common destiny.

Certainly, the whole idea of an end is problematic and must be seen metaphorically because it is ultimately an artificial construct. Nothing actually ends in a transformational Universe. Science speculates that reality is process shaped, eternally renewing itself within a multi-Universe structure that continuously contracts and expands into new worlds. That may or may not be so, yet within our world in time we can detect the shape of a story that began with the Big Bang and is now deep into the rising action or even the falling action. Perhaps we could describe it as a story within a story within a story and so on. The endings I am speaking of are the end of each life, the end of the manifest Cosmos, and the end of temporal reality within this realm. The point that I really want to make here is that I believe in a happy ending for our world that is reflected in the world of literature.

There is an understanding in literary circles that neat, happy endings indicate the superficiality of both the story and the author in question. This is rightly so because, as we all know, life just does not happen like that. For a start, there is no such thing as a true ending in this life because the next moment brings more change, and even happy resolutions give way to yet further problems to be overcome. Good stories do not provide an artificial resolution to all of life's difficulties, but they touch a place deep in the human psyche that aches for completion. I submit that every one of us has an urgent if submerged longing for a happy ending; ultimate peace and contentment; consummate victory of good over evil; a destination for the long, arduous journey; an arrival at our true home (that we will never have to leave); an end to all goodbyes. My hunch is that these feelings are not just immature fantasies symptomatic of our inability to accept reality as it is, but reliable barometers of our destiny and the future of the Universe. The compass needle within each human being (I cannot speak for other creatures) is insistently drawn to the Omega Point. Whenever we read a great piece of literature, we experience a tremendous stab of grief at the end, partly because we can no longer live with those characters in that world, but partly because we empathize with the pathos of their continuing lives within the struggle of existence. We desperately want them to be home and safe and finally happy. Literature mirrors the human heart. For now we all have to live with the joys and pains of incompleteness, but the good news that I want to propose in this chapter is that a warm hearth does await us at the end of the journey and this knowledge fills each passing moment with joy.

NOW AND NOT YET

It is almost blasphemy these days to speak about a future orientation—we are supposed to all be focused on the now, not the pie-in-the-sky future. For myself, I think that this favoring of the present moment, although it has contributed greatly to current spiritualities, is an over-reaction to a traditional thinking that totally ignored the present or saw it as a place of suffering that must be endured in order to get the reward of a blissful future after death. Authors such as Eckhart Tolle say that if we could live entirely in the present moment, we would be already achieving the bliss of eternal reality.[5] I find myself readily agreeing with him that we can taste the joy and contentment of what is truly real right now, and that we would be foolish not to immerse ourselves as much as possible in that bliss, but I am also reminded of the realized eschatology I learnt about in my theology classes—that heaven can be tasted now within the tension of the now and the not yet, but cannot be fully realized in the present. In Tolle's writing, I miss the 'not yet.' I do not believe that anyone can acquire a state of mind that allows him or her to bypass the opposing tensions of the Universe. Even the most enlightened guru who has mastered the art of indifference to joy and sorrow must still live day to day on this Earth and, therefore, cannot be completely in bliss. Nirvana is not in this realm. The holiest saints within Christendom, like John of the Cross, experience the exquisite torture of being so close to becoming love that only the thin veil of death separates them from God. It is the 'not yet' that increases our longing.

Perhaps there is another fine balance we could achieve by living the mixed blessings of the current moment with as much zest and gusto as possible while keeping our eye on a future of blissful resolution. It is my contention that the former is not really possible without the latter. I should speak for myself. Even though I am constantly amazed and thrilled at the beauty of this life on this Earth, it only increases my appetite to taste life fully in a way not possible within the tensions of the present moment. I cannot live today with real joy, without believing that it is all going somewhere—that one day I will be in a consummate relationship with the reality I can only taste now—that one day I will be completely happy. For me, that is the promise of the story of life that lives within the story of God.

5. Tolle, *Power of Now.*

14

Is Nature Immortal?

I HAVE ALREADY GIVEN a clear indication of where my own beliefs about our destiny lie, but I want to look respectfully and carefully at the spirituality that rejects an afterlife and espouses the belief that at death we simply return to the Earth. To do this, I refer to David Suzuki and to my father-in-law who has come to a certain peace in his old age about his future place in the Universe.

NO TRANSCENDENCE IS NECESSARY

Suzuki is influenced by the worldview of his parents who followed the ancient Shinto religion of Japan and also by his lifelong dedication to environmentalism and deep ecology. A brief look at the tenets of Shinto illuminates his perspective. This nature religion recognizes no dualism in the world. There is no separation of body and spirit, and there is no transcendent realm outside the natural world. Everything is part of one unified Cosmos. Spirit beings and Gods do exist but not in a separate realm; they are part of the invisible world, which is an extension of the visible world we are aware of. The whole natural Universe is considered sacred. Thus Suzuki derives all the meaning he needs from the Universe itself, which is the true home of every living being. We arise from the Earth at birth, and at death we return home to our place in creation.[1] Suzuki rejects the existence of a transcendent realm because all our longings for immortality are met in the material Universe. Looking back over the eons, we can see that the matter erupting from the Big Bang is still with us, transformed into stars, planets, rocks, vegetation, animals, and our own bodies: "Matter is not mortal . . . matter is not transitory, it is transformational; it moves

1. Suzuki, *Sacred Balance*, 195.

through time and space from form to form, but it is never lost."² When we die, the Earth reclaims our portion of itself—we live on in nature and in our descendents. There is no other meaning or purpose to life: "What is the meaning of life? Answer: life. Why are we here? Answer: to be here, to be-long, to be."³ Therefore, humans should throw all of their energy and creativity into contributing to the beauty of the Earth and to repairing the damage we have caused through ignorance and greed.

Suzuki illustrates his perspective by two stories about the death of family members. They both speak of the dead continuing to exist through nature and, in particular, through children and grandchildren. I include them here in his own words:

> A clematis plant has climbed along the back gate. When my mother died, we scattered her ashes on it, and when my sister's daughter died, we added some of her ashes to Grandma's. Now when the purple flowers bloom, the pain of the loss of my mother and niece is softened because I feel they are nearby.⁴

Obituary, May 8, 1994:

> Carr Kaoru Suzuki [David Suzuki's father] died peacefully on May 8. He was eighty-five. His ashes will be spread on the winds of Quadra Island. He found great strength in the Japanese tradition of nature-worship. Shortly before he died, he said: 'I will return to nature where I came from. I will be part of the fish, the trees, the birds—that's my reincarnation. I have had a rich and full life and have no regrets. I will live on in your memories of me and through my grandchildren.'⁵

Along these same lines, I had an interesting and enlightening conversation a while ago with my father-in-law, Dave Anderson. He told me that he had tried for many years to immerse himself within the Christian mindset, including life after death with its heaven or hell. However, he confessed that he had never fully internalized it and felt somewhat distant from the traditional belief in an afterlife. He said, "It did not really fit what I truly believed—it did not really make sense to me. I accepted Christianity because it was expected of me within my family, and I tried my best to be

2. Ibid., 206.
3. Ibid., 206.
4. Ibid., 205.
5. Ibid., 198.

a good Christian. Now that I am old, I no longer feel the need to conform to this spirituality. When I look back over my life, I can see that the time I have spent immersed in nature has formed my deepest beliefs about life and death. Nature has been my true church where I have felt close to God. I no longer believe in an afterlife for myself. I look around me when I am out taking photos of nature and see that everything dies and returns to the Earth. That is all I want—to be one with the natural world that I came from. All the plants and animals around me are going to die and dissolve back into the Earth, and I do not see why it should be any different for me. It just makes sense. It gives me a sense of peace to think about it."

After this conversation, I experienced certain turmoil inside myself. I felt very attracted to this spirituality; it seemed so right and so true. Christian claims for an afterlife appeared fantastic and unlikely against the refreshing common sense and simplicity of this approach. What particularly pricked me was his reference to the other creatures of this world. Why does Christianity only seem to have an eternal fate for human beings? What about the rest of creation? Well, the familiar traditional arguments come to mind: only human beings have souls that make them immortal; everything else will simply die and return to the Earth. This does not ring true with the ideas of the new cosmology, which suggest that all of nature has an inner dimension—a growing consciousness that is simply the most developed in human beings. In this sense, the entire world has a soul. In any case, I deeply believe that the fate of human beings is one with that of the Cosmos. We are on a journey together. In that, I wholeheartedly concur with Dave, but I cannot believe, as he does, that life is a cyclical repetition of birth and death that continues on without arriving anywhere and with no particular purpose. I am not sure I have ever felt entirely at home in this life, and I cannot still a restless probing for a transcendent horizon. I think another realm is our true home. My spirit strains toward a state beyond nature, beyond the current laws of the Universe. What lies at the heart of my conviction that there is an existence beyond the laws of nature is the fidelity of God. I cannot believe that perfect love could leave the world continuing on forever bound within the polarities of current existence. The promises of God declare something more.

SCIENCE AND THE FUTURE

Perhaps this is a good place to look at what science is speculating about with regards to the far future. We do not know whether matter is immortal or not. Certainly, it has existed for a very long time and manifested itself in countless transformations, but despite its longevity perhaps it too will disappear one day. As it rose from mystery at the beginning of time, so it will, perhaps, return there when the world has run its course. The end of the Earth seems to be a sure thing—if it survives that long, it will be destroyed after five billion years or so when the Sun enters its red dwarf stage of dying. Planet Earth will first become like an enormous greenhouse—a global jungle, and then dry out, bursting into flames and becoming a desiccated desert until the rocks themselves melt, and finally, the winds from the dying Sun will blow the planet apart and scatter its remains into the Cosmos, to be picked up again as the building material for another planet. However, this constant rebuilding of solar systems seems to stretch into infinity. Or does it? Some scientists adhere to the theory of a closed Universe, where the current expansion will eventually peter out, and a huge gravitational pull will collapse the Cosmos back into itself like a fiery reversal of the Big Bang. On the other hand, there is the theory of the open Universe where the gravitational pull is thought to be not strong enough to draw back the Cosmos, and therefore, it continues to expand, with bodies of matter getting further and further away from each other and the heat of the Cosmos dissipating more and more. It seems the Universe will die from heat or from cold. However, there may not be a final end to the Cosmos. Some scientists foresee an eternity of expansion and contraction—many Universes coming into being and then returning to mystery, like the inhalation and exhalation of some giant being. As well, quantum physics has shown us that matter itself is not some dead inert substance directed by external forces, but it is energy—self-perpetuating, self-organizing, transformative energy that is both manifest and unmanifest.

We move deep into complexity and mystery as we contemplate the Cosmos as both manifest and unmanifest. The Universe itself may have some of the attributes Western religion has reserved for God. In fact, liberal Christianity has come to see the Universe as part of God in what it describes as panentheism. If traditional Christianity sees the Universe and God as separate, and pantheism sees them as identical, panentheism suggests that the Universe is part of God in a similar way to the body being part of the whole person. God transcends the Cosmos, yet the Cosmos is truly a part of God. Perhaps we can talk about realms of existence within one united whole that is God. This relationship of creation to God is, in the end, beyond all our categories and even beyond all metaphors and powers of symbolization. For the purposes of this chapter, what is important to me is to explore what may lie ahead of this realm of existence that we know as life on planet Earth within the space-time that we now experience. In particular, I want to make a case for there being a resolution phase to this cosmic manifestation, one that we have traditionally called heaven.

The next thinkers we shall look at to help us on our quest are process theologians. They are panentheist in their orientation and see a continual flow of movement from this realm of experience into a pan-cosmic existence of unity with God into eternity. Their views are characterized by open-endedness and a continuation of the basic laws of the known Universe and, therefore, do not offer any resolution to the polarities that currently shape existence. They look at the shape of reality as we know it now and take their clues about the eschatological future from that. Within the contours of this chapter they fall into the continuity category. They propose the existence of an afterlife, but one that continues along the same lines as this world.

PROCESS THEOLOGY

As its name suggests, process theology is based on the idea of continual change. In this system there is no sense of existence coming to an ultimate fulfillment that is beyond the current polarities of the Cosmos. The idea of reality ever becoming static, even in heaven, is unthinkable. As process theologian Ian Barbour argues, "God's goal is not the completed achievement of a static final realm, but rather a continuing advance toward richer and more harmonious relationships."[6] This sounds very exciting, but it becomes apparent that within process thought this also means continuing suffering as a necessary component of growth and development. In a world of continuity, where there is no end to enrichment, there is no end to pain. Also, it is not clear in process theology if immortality refers to anything or anybody except God. Each entity (process language is sci-

6. Barbour, *Age of Science*, chap. 8, sec. 4.

entific and impersonal), which is the sum of its experiences, occupies a span of time and space within existence but then at death ceases to have 'actual occasions of experience' and passes into God. The subjectivity of an entity does not survive, but the values that have been existentially realized by that entity attain an objective immortality in the memory of God. In other language one could say that God saves all that is possible to save from an entity's life, all that is worthy of being saved, in God's own being. Ian Barbour puts it this way: "Every entity is valuable for its ongoing contribution to the life of God. The values achieved in this world are preserved in God's eternal life, and this is part of their enduring significance and permanence beyond the flux of time."[7] Process thought speaks about entities in order to include all cosmic subjects, not just human beings, but necessarily, much of this philosophy is centered on human experience. Henceforth we will focus on humans, keeping in mind the wider applicability that is needed to reflect on the future in cosmic terms.

Process theology submits that there is no immortal part of human beings that remains after death. As process theologian Norman Pittenger says, "All of us do die; that we know. And all of us does die."[8] He suggests that the concept of an immortal soul arose from the human desire to escape the finality of total death. In his opinion, humans would do better to allow that finality to create an urgency to live well, contributing whatever they can to "the ongoing creative advance of the Cosmos."[9] In this, he and Swimme sound very similar.

It seems that there is a fair amount of dissention and confusion about eschatological matters within process theology circles. Some thinkers defend objective immortality, which we have already seen is our participation in God's eternal nature, and some propose subjective immortality, "in which the human self continues as a center of experience in a radically different environment but amid continuing change rather than a changeless eternity."[10] In the former scenario the individual is assimilated entirely into God; in the latter scenario there is a sense of the continuation of the individual self within God, but not in the traditional sense that the self experiences unending bliss because it is still caught in the polarities

7. Ibid., chap. 5, sec. 4.

8. Pittenger, 'Last Things,' chap. 3, para. 12.

9. Ibid., chap. 3, para. 14.

10. Barbour, *Age of Science*, chap. 8, sec. 4.

of process. Process theologians such as Charles Hartshorne and Schubert Ogden suggest that it is simply egotistical and a lack of abandonment to God that causes the desire for subjective immortality, yet the implications of both the continued suffering of God and the lack of fulfillment for human beings and all other entities raise serious questions for any ideology that seeks for a happy ending to the story.

It appears that within process theology God remains eternally on the cross, united with the struggling Cosmos, which never finally reaches Easter Sunday, laboring with the world for a birth that never arrives. And for human beings and the rest of creation—is it never possible to taste the exquisiteness of a joy that is not tinged with sadness? Do we never get to heaven—or if we do, do we know anything about it?

These thinkers argue for the continuation of change and development into eternity. Nothing ever comes to a place where God is all in all because there is forever an ongoing process of entities gaining their moment, their span in cosmic space-time, during which they strive to develop as much as possible and feed that growth into God who is changing all the time. God is growing in process theology as a direct result of the choices made within space-time. God and creation are not separate, but different parts of one being. Thus God's experience is our experience; we are the experience of God. Without us God could not grow and change, and so God is dependent on evolving creation. Our pains and joys are God's pains and joys. For our purposes in this chapter, it is important to note that these qualities continue on without resolution forever. That means that God is always achieving further reaches of beauty but at the cost of suffering. The polarities existing within space-time and giving rise to the struggles and achievements of existence continue in tension, never reaching any final synthesis.

Within this system of thought, the idea of heaven takes on very different characteristics than are found within a traditional Christian framework. Psychologist and theologian Diarmuid O'Murchu describes this kind of heaven in his book *Quantum Theology*. I do not know whether he would consider himself a process thinker, but his heaven is very like one that could emerge from process theology. He also is concerned with respecting continuity with the existing parameters of the Cosmos and the dynamics that order temporal existence. This means accepting a continuation of suffering in heaven for the sake of ongoing creativity and further development. He puts it this way: "Heaven . . . refers to that harmonious state of being whereby we enjoy a permanent sense of attunement with the progressive, eternal nature of evolution itself . . . The belief that heaven is a state of absolute happiness may be something of a misnomer . . . A sense of being eternally attuned to life does not mean escaping all pain and suffering, but rather being empowered to participate more holistically in the mixture of agony and ecstasy which has characterized evolution from time immemorial."[11]

O'Murchu follows the subjective immortality proposed by some process theologians—that the self continues on in some way after death as part of the constantly evolving deity. Arriving at this kind of heaven is the only logical conclusion to the continuity model that embraces evolution and process both in this life and the next. For myself, I can respect the effort to come up with a seamless theology that takes seriously the panentheistic belief that the world is part of God. It honors the Cosmos as truly revelatory of the nature of God and makes a stand against dualistic thinking that is easily dismissive of space-time existence. However, it leaves me terribly disappointed that love is never completely triumphant, and the goal of existence is further struggle, albeit a higher more harmonious struggle. Of course, its great advantage is that it finally gets rid of the notion of a static heaven where bored angels float around on clouds. Is there a way to have my cake and eat it—to have a dynamic heaven and to eliminate pain and suffering? I believe there is, and to find it we need to move to the next model, which is that of continuity-discontinuity.

11. O'Murchu, *Quantum Theology*, 170.

15

Continuity and Discontinuity

THE ULTIMATE DESTINY OF the Universe is to preserve its essential integrity within a transformed realm where ever-increasing richness is not concomitant with struggle. John Polkinghorne, who is a scientist as well as a theologian, has done some work in this area, and the book he co-edited with Michael Welker, *The End of the World and the Ends of God*, is very helpful. Polkinghorne and Welker note that the abiding theme running through the eschatological discussions contained in the volume is one of continuity and discontinuity. In terms of the ends of God and the Universe, there will be similarities to the present contours of existence and great differences as the world undergoes a kind of metamorphosis in reaching its final goal.

A NEW CREATION

Although he might be criticized for speculating too boldly about the nature of the eschatological future, Polkinghorne is courageous in challenging the conclusions of process theology regarding immortality and the fulfillment of God's promises. Personally, I find his attempt to reconcile cosmology with traditional Christian concepts is not always helpful and seems rather strained at times. Nevertheless, I find myself in agreement with the broad scope of his ideas. He argues for a transformed creation that will forever explore the perfection of love. This new creation promised by God will not be another creation from nothing, as Christian theology describes the birth of the Cosmos, but will be a transformation of the existing Universe.

Polkinghorne and Welker argue that science and religion deal with one and the same reality, and therefore religious ideas about the future of the world are not "a wild 'leap of faith' against all we know about the

Universe. On the contrary, the assumption of their existence is warranted by what we already know about the Universe."[1]

Against the backdrop of impending disaster for the Universe, caused either by the burning death of a 'big crunch' or the cold death of gradual entropy, Polkinghorne and Welker ask if it is theology's job to contrive fantasies that will help humans feel better. Belief in an afterlife along with the Christian concept of heaven has been accused of being exactly that—just a nice story to make a happy ending that makes people feel better about death. However, they dismiss these criticisms by insisting that faith in the promises of God is rooted in the same reality that science speaks about.

Also, Polkinghorne challenges process ideas that suggest that objective immortality is all that human beings can hope for. A major concern for him is for humans not only to be preserved in the memory of God, not only survive in the experiences they contribute to God, but to be resurrected and become new embodied beings. He preserves the Christian teaching of resurrection of the body: "It would seem a coherent hope that this vastly complex pattern that is a human person could, at death, be held in the divine mind to await its reembodiment within the life of the world to come."[2] The preservation of patterns is at the heart of his thinking. He states, "Where the continuity between the two worlds can be expected to be expressed is in a carry over of pattern . . . The pattern which is each person or thing in the Universe continues on."[3] There will be discontinuity in the transformed Universe because the patterns undergo metamorphosis in a way that is unexpected and incomprehensible from our present vantage point, and also, the future realm will not be a continuation of current cosmic polarities. The entire Universe is transformed in the same way, not just human beings. Somehow, the physical matter of this world will be transformed into a resurrected world, and there provide the bodily material for new life, for God will no more abandon the Universe than his human children.

Therefore, Polkinghorne challenges the notion that the dynamics of this present world continue into the next, where change, and therefore suffering, is forever a part of the make-up of reality. He insists that the

1. Polkinghorne and Welker, *End of World*, 4.
2. Polkinghorne, "Eschatology," 39.
3. Ibid., 39.

laws governing the Cosmos as we know it will be different in a transformed Universe: "In our world, the cost of the evolution of novelty is the certainty of its impermanence. If the world to come is to be free from death and suffering, its "matter-energy" will have to be given a different character. There will have to be a discontinuous change of physical law."[4] The big question that arises from this discontinuity is—if we lose the creative tension produced by our current physical laws, will the transformed realm lose all the wonder and adventure we have enjoyed in space-time existence, along with the struggle and suffering we would be quite happy to leave behind?

EVER-DEEPENING LOVE

Will there be change and novelty in heaven? Will beauty fade away without the dynamic forces of chaos and determinism fuelling its continued radiance? One might suppose that Polkinghorne's heaven is a static and boring anti-climax to the adventure of space-time living. However, he proposes that the perfection of the heavenly realm will be dynamic and ongoing. The chief difference between his heaven and the eternity proposed by process theology is that his does not involve change through the introduction of novelty, which causes such suffering in the present. For him the transformed Universe is perfect but not static. He suggests that the notion of perfection derived from Plato must give way to the idea of a dynamic, increasing fulfillment that involves only an ever-deepening experience of love: "We need to rid ourselves of the vestiges of the platonic notion that perfection is static, and to replace it with an altogether more dynamic concept . . . It is the exploration of the endless variations of divine perfection that will constitute the harmony of the heavenly realm."[5] These ideas come closer to a satisfactory notion of an afterlife for me. I agree with Polkinghorne's assertion that the promises of God offer more than objective immortality. It is difficult to imagine how each particle of Earthly existence is carried forward into transformed existence in heaven, with the essence or pattern of each thing being brought to its own completion, and yet it rings true to me that the source and creator of all that is would bring us all home into harmonious fulfillment. My old holy card echoes again: "Nothing is lost, and all in the end is harvest."

4. Ibid., 39.

5. Polkinghorne, *God of Hope*, 120.

Somehow, the mysterious presence of each entity will keep its identity within the unity of love.

Heaven is not just for people but also for the whole transformed Cosmos. For me this vision grants a blessing on the multitude of lives struggling upward toward the fullness of life and love. Each effort and sacrifice to become more is not lost but rewarded by God with greater being. The human heroes who went before us, whom we hold in such esteem for their tremendous self-giving, for their striving for justice and compassion, did not lose their essential selves at death but live on in transformed existence in the heart of God. Mahatma Gandhi, Martin Luther King Jr., Dietrich Bonhoeffer, Dian Fossey, Rosa Parks, Francis of Assisi—and all the unknown heroes who have struggled in honesty and integrity for greater life—are cheering us on, encouraging us forward toward our own completion. This is what the communion of saints means to me.

HEAVEN IS A GREAT FEAST

Brian Swimme urges us all to become heroes, to live our lives in such a way as to become food for the great feast of heaven. He borrows this analogy partly from an African tribal perspective and partly from his Christian roots where Jesus often refers to heaven as a great feast everyone is invited to come to and celebrate there the triumph of love into eternity. Doesn't sound too boring to me! Swimme says that humans will only be able to pass into eternity if they live lives that are ennobling. The Universe is the place for becoming God's food, real food. Enduring the terror of loss and learning to give themselves away in love is required in order for humans to become interesting food and join the feast: "To live a life is to create a feast. It is an ongoing sacrificial event. Our lives should be devoted to an understanding that our destiny is to participate in the feast."[6] The Universe saves everything of value, everything that can be saved. Evil, as Swimme presents it, is a shrinking and reduction that becomes nothing at all in the light of eternity. It cannot become real. Evil lives are not interesting to eat, not appetizing. Goodness is everything that contributes to the life of the Cosmos, and evil is everything that destroys it. Swimme urges humans to ask what they can produce that will activate life. What can they do with their small amount of time and energy to contribute to the great feast? What gift can the human species unfold into the great adventure?

6. Swimme, *Canticle to Cosmos*, 5

The corollary of this is that unloving acts and totally selfish people just disappear—they cannot survive into eternity. In religious terms one could say that hell in this sense is non-existence. However, I suspect that many of us have become real enough to squeak through, and God is kind enough to recognize our efforts and allow us to continue the journey to full reality beyond the realm of space-time. Maybe this is what purgatory is all about—the old Catholic idea that has become so unpopular could take on new life within this cosmology. It would need to lose the symbolism surrounding it in the past—rattling chains and imprisonment for the debt unpaid on Earth! These concepts will take on more meaning toward the end of this chapter as C. S. Lewis takes us on an imaginary trip to the beautiful land of heaven.

16

Promise, Hope, and the Journey Home

THE WORDS PROMISE AND *hope* have been given a strong theological treatment by Jürgen Moltmann, and I am indebted to him for the roots of this chapter's ideas. However, rather than focusing on Moltmann's developed eschatology, we will be looking at John Haught's ideas on the destiny of the Cosmos. Haught has taken Moltmann's thought and applied it to the vision of the new cosmology, which makes him a very useful contributor to this chapter.

Hope and promise are highly evocative, emotional words for all humans, giving a heady, intoxicating glow to the brain and a tingle of anticipation to the solar plexus. However, one could argue—and Moltmann does—that Christians experience the thrill of these words more keenly than others because their entire religious vision is contained within them. They are words that strain forward toward the future. Christianity is a radically–future-oriented religion. The kingdom promised by Jesus is present in seed form, but it is growing into a mighty tree in the future.[1] It is the modicum of yeast that will produce a sumptuous loaf for the banquet.[2] It is now and it is not yet—Christianity lives in the delicious tension of what is now and what is to come in the future. It lends itself well to an evolutionary vision where the Universe is journeying toward a consummate destiny, filling out and growing up as it goes.

However, this future orientation has got Christianity into a lot of trouble in the past. Promise and hope reach for the future but have to be grounded in the present or they develop into a caricature of Christianity that ignores both the good that currently exists, and also the struggle forward that is necessary to bring about the fullness of the kingdom. What

1. Mark 4:30–32 (NRSV).
2. Matt. 13:33 (NRSV).

results from this is a passive otherworldly spirituality that urges the human race to put up with the pains and injustices of life because those who are good will receive pie in the sky by and by. This is so different from what Jesus lived and preached.

THE URGENT ESCHATOLOGY OF JESUS

Rather than being passive in the face of suffering and injustice, Jesus railed against it. The urgency of Jesus' kingdom vision strained toward a future that could only be realized through nurturing the seeds of compassion and justice in the human heart in the present moment. He urged his disciples to understand that the kingdom was among them and within them.[3] It is already now and it is growing to majestic fullness, but it is not some automatic thing that God is doing to helpless humanity; it must be chosen and lived radically to be accomplished. I think if Jesus had been alive at the same time as Teilhard de Chardin, he would have commended his belief that the heavenly realm, the kingdom of God, can only come about through the transformation of the Cosmos into love.

Jesus radiated hope through his declaration of the promises of God. The God of Jesus is characterized by extravagance, surprise, and superabundance. Our boats are suddenly overflowing with fish after a night of fruitless labor;[4] like the tardy vineyard worker, we are heaped with more reward than we have earned;[5] we discover that nobody is excluded from the feast despite our apparent unworthiness.[6] The only appropriate response to this promising God is hope, which abandons the human heart to trust in the giver of such overwhelming, freely given bounty: "Hope is a radical, unquestioning openness to the breaking in of God's future."[7]

Eschatology is not only a study of the last things—that is to say, death and the life beyond death—but it is concerned with hope in the goodness of a future vision, grounded in what is real in the present. Hope is demanding; it requires a continual relinquishing of the present in order to receive the future. It calls us ever deeper into adventure—fully living the present moment while straining toward the future. Passivity is not a pos-

---

3. Luke 17:21 (NRSV).

4. John 21:1–14 (NRSV).

5. Matt. 20:1–16 (NRSV).

6. Matt. 22:2–14 (NRSV).

7. Haught, *Mystery and Promise*, chap. 5, para. 24.

sibility because the future is only built on the work of the present: "Hope realizes that the arrival of the future requires our energetic involvement in its coming. Hope withers when it loses its connection to nature, to time and place, and to the need for action here and now."[8] Hope is only real because it is grounded in love.

John Haught speaks of Jesus as the compassion of God who suffers with the world on its way toward realization. Jesus cried with humans and railed against all the natural and manmade adversity that human existence is plagued by. He expressed an urgency to do away with it as soon as possible. He gave voice again to the God of Israel, rescuing the people in their need, especially the most marginalized. He manifested an "exceptionally intense compassion for the needy, the poor, the outcasts, the guilt ridden, and the forgotten whom he encountered every day. His longing to remove their misery compelled him to announce that the God of Moses . . . was now once again near at hand and ready to rescue the people from their pain."[9] Haught submits that Jesus radiated an impatient eschatology because the future of God's reign was pressing in, and he knew how much more was possible for life. He passionately threw himself into the task of awakening humanity to the good news of the marvelous destiny that was theirs to claim: "Jesus understood his public vocation to be that of announcing the limitless breadth of the divine vision."[10] At times he showed his frustration at the disciples and the people of his time for not grasping his message. It was not until after Jesus' death that this vision started to enter their awareness and awaken their own passion for the realization of the kingdom.

Jesus, along with other incarnations of divine love throughout history, announced and lived the promises of God. He reassures us that our lives are not caught in a meaningless cycle of pleasure and pain going nowhere. He blesses every effort to grow in love, promising that they will not be lost but will speed the realization of the kingdom. But this kingdom is not only the fulfillment of God's promise to the human race, it is also the destiny of the whole Cosmos. Haught points out that theology has usually seen Scripture only in relation to human redemption but, "[r]evelation

---

8. Ibid., chap. 5, para. 30.
9. Ibid., chap. 6, para. 27.
10. Ibid., chap. 6, para. 38.

must now be interpreted as God's envisagement of the *whole Universe's* possibilities and ultimate destiny."[11]

COMPREHENSIVE REVELATION

A quick revisit of the loaded word *revelation* might be helpful here. Revelation speaks of the desire of God to be known in creation and of God's will to communicate with the world. As we have seen, Swimme and Berry declare that the primary revelation of the divine is the Universe itself. We know God through the Cosmos, which reveals divine attributes because it is actually a part of God. However, Haught modifies their statement by arguing that the fullness of revelation comes not only from the perceived reality of the emerging Universe, but also from faith developed by the particular communication of God to the human race. Coming from a Christian perspective, Haught speaks only of biblical revelation, but this could be broadened to include the revelatory visions of all religions, and indeed to all receptive people throughout history. Human revelation is a story within the wider narrative of cosmic history where the seed of God was first planted: "The cosmos itself, having come into being eons before the arrival of human history, is the more encompassing context of God's self-revelation . . . Yet faith allows us to read cosmic events in the light of the revelatory promises of God that occur within our terrestrially bound human history. In the light of Christian faith, we may even say that billions of years before biblical religion emerged on Earth the Universe had already been seeded with promise."[12]

The revelation of God through the Universe comes to us primarily through the work of science, which Berry has described as a sustained meditation on the Cosmos. The particular revelation to the human race has come primarily through the sacred scriptures of the world's religions. Both science and religion however, are limited by their own processes and cannot produce a comprehensive picture of reality by themselves. Both are needed to perceive the depths of God's promise. Science and theology depend on each other to produce a rich synthesis of where the Universe is going. Without science, theology would not understand the nature of the evolving world, how it was 'born' and what its patterns of emergence have been. Nor would it understand how the continuation of those patterns

11. Ibid., chap. 8, para. 5.

12. Ibid., chap. 8, para. 3.

might flow into the fulfillment of the promises of God. Without theology, science is like a bereft child, not knowing where home is. It is left with the knowledge that the Universe is either going to burn up or drift apart one day, without the hope that there is a saving presence able to bring the Cosmos to fulfillment.

What then, is the promise made by God to the evolving Universe? From what has been said, it would be natural to conclude that it is the same promise made to humans through the explicit revelation of the sacred scriptures. In the manner of Swimme and Berry, one could say that through religion, the Universe is declaring its own possibilities, dreaming of its own potential. Haught does not try to make predictions about what the ultimate destiny of the Universe is, but believes the Cosmos will find its own fulfillment within the extravagant surprises of God: "From the moment of its creation nature, too, even apart from human existence, has felt the promise of God . . . persuading the Cosmos to reach for further and more intense modes of fulfillment."[13] As we turn now to ponder the mystery of what Haught calls cosmic homelessness, it becomes possible to suggest that the promise involves the Cosmos finding itself finally at home.

COSMIC HOMELESSNESS

Haught begins by asking the question that arises from the human experience of alienation: "Why is it we often do not feel truly at home in this Universe?"[14] Since primal pantheistic practices gave way to the major religions we embrace today, there has been a growing sense of alienation between the human race and the natural world that has led to the feeling of not being at home in the Universe. Our early ancestors experienced themselves as undifferentiated from the Earth which gave them birth and nourishment, yet the climb to greater consciousness produced the experience of differentiation. Perhaps this was an inevitable part of growing up, but this alienation was also caused by dualistic philosophy, which separated Earth and heaven, body and soul, matter and spirit, provoking a disregard for Earthly existence. Within Christian theology the faithful were taught to look down on the material and elevate the spiritual: "Religions and philosophies of the East and West, at least since the axial age, have

13. Ibid., chap. 8, para. 25.
14. Ibid., chap. 8, para. 41.

at times made us feel alien to the natural world. They have convinced us that we are strangers in a foreign land to which we do not really belong. At times they have even led us to a hatred of the Earth. They give us the impression that authentic existence involves a sense of being exiled from the Cosmos."[15]

As we have already seen, Swimme broadens the blame for this experience of exile from the Universe by including the mechanistic materialism promoted by science, which has taught the human race to view the Universe as a collection of dead objects or resources to be used, then discarded at will. Humans have lost their sense of the interrelatedness of everything in the Cosmos and no longer understand their place in the web of life. They forget that their very bodies are made up of the elemental particles that were forged in the fireball and existed as stars eons before they became knitted in human flesh. Swimme wants humans to be able to look out at the vastness of a starry night sky and feel at home because they understand they are related to everything they see.

I have to admit I experience a struggle with feeling really at home in the Cosmos. Immersed in the urban throng of people going about the busy living of their lives on planet Earth, I feel nestled somewhat in the familiar web of humankind. However, when I am out in the countryside, far way from human habitat, feelings of alienation creep in around my deep appreciation of the beautiful world. Everything whispers to me of otherness, of the evolution of nature, of where I have come from and where I am going. Belonging is there, but so is alienation. The night sky affects me even more strangely, eliciting awe at the majestic size of the Universe, but also a kind of horror at all that empty space. No doubt part of my experience could be linked to the dualistic philosophy I have imbibed for most of my life, but I believe it also points to a recognition of the journey aspect of life. In the end, I agree with my Christian roots that the Cosmos is not my final home. Although I am a child of the Cosmos, I am not fully at home here because the Cosmos itself is on a journey home.

Haught speaks eloquently of the pilgrim nature of life as one of the central tenets of Christianity. Temporal existence cannot fully hold all the promises of God, and homelessness is part of the human experience, a necessary part that hastens the pilgrimage home. He suggests that the best balance to reach this side of eternity is to be at home but not fully

15. Ibid., chap. 8, para. 42.

at home. The Bible is full of examples of this exodus mentality, and Jesus' life and teachings urge us to not fit in too comfortably with any present actuality. Haught captures well the decisive reason for embracing homelessness: "However, faith promotes homelessness not as an end in itself but as a necessary moment in the quest for our true home guaranteed by God's revelatory promise . . . it resists our settling for something as home which is really not an adequate domicile for our hope. According to the biblical vision, nothing less than the inexhaustible futurity of God can be the appropriate destiny of the human spirit."[16] He goes on to propose that the deeper reason why humans do not feel at home in the Cosmos is that the Universe itself is on a journey to completion. He is indebted to Moltmann for these ideas, which are taken from the theology of the Sabbath in *God in Creation*.

Haught agrees with Moltmann that the Universe is continually restless as it probes forward to find its ultimate form. It becomes possible to say that the restless yearning of human beings is a further, more developed expression of the restlessness of the whole Universe. We are incomplete because the Universe is incomplete, and we journey on together to find our way home. The Universe is "akin to a fellow traveler that has begun the journey of responding to revelation's promise epochs before we ourselves arrived on the scene to join it."[17] God's promises are not limited to humans but are made to the entire body of creation. As we read in the letter to the Romans: "We know that the whole creation has been groaning in labor pains until now."[18] The urgency of imminent birth is upon us all as we struggle toward greater life and the consummation of love. St. Paul also told us that what we take for reality now is like a dim reflection of what is to come, and together with the whole Universe we strain toward a face-to-face existence with God.[19]

16. Ibid., chap. 8, para. 51.
17. Ibid., chap. 8, para. 54.
18. Rom. 8:22 (NRSV).
19. 1 Cor. 13:12 (NRSV).

17

Toward Omega

F OR THE MOST PART, the vision of the far future and end times have been treated by the scholars examined in this study with a certain delicate vagueness, no doubt in order to maintain a respectful agnosticism about that which no one should dare to pontificate upon. This surely is very wise, yet within this humble openness, the imagination can play boldly. With this in mind we turn back to Teilhard de Chardin whose mystic intuition of what is to come thrills the human spirit with dreams of fulfillment.

In order to grasp what Teilhard is saying about the future of the Universe, one needs to understand his ideas about the nature and direction of cosmic evolution, so we will briefly revisit these before we go on. As we proceed, it is also important to keep in mind that Teilhard was attempting to reconcile his own scientific understandings with the eschatological doctrine of the Catholic Church due to the tremendous pressure he was under to conform. He wove his spirituality around established teachings, and therefore, he maintained the basic framework of an end of the world, or Parousia, brought about by the second coming of Christ. His conclusions certainly did not find favor with Rome, but they offer profound and provocative conjecture about the mystery of God's future. Teilhard was not afraid to be bold in his speculation about the direction and destiny of the Universe, and this led to him being marginalized by both science and theology. Although he was a renowned paleontologist, many of his ideas seem to flow from intuition—which as far as I am concerned is as valid a way of proceeding as any other. It did not do Einstein any harm.

CONVERGENCE TOWARD UNITY

The best place to begin is with Teilhard's law of complexity-consciousness, which asserted that from the beginning, the direction of life was from simplicity to complexity and that higher consciousness accompanied greater complexity. The pattern of evolving life was similar to a branching tree, continually probing forward to find new avenues for the emergence of novelty and increasing consciousness. However, Teilhard saw that this direction toward pluralism did not continue on indefinitely and that evolution reached a turning point where, instead of straining outward, it folded back on itself and began a journey toward unification. A climax was reached at the emergence of human beings, and then life turned inward, seeking further development through human consciousness, and began a unifying course of convergence toward a central point that he named the Omega Point. Teilhard described it this way: "Pluralism, far from being the ultimate end of evolution, is merely a first outspreading whose gradual shrinkage displays the true curve of Nature's proceedings. Essentially the Universe is narrowing to a centre, like the successive layers of a cone: it is *convergent* in structure."[1]

Through the inwardness of human self-reflexive consciousness, the world continues to evolve and will discover ever-greater degrees of unity. Teilhard saw a time when the collective mind of the human race, which he called the noosphere would develop a kind of thinking web around the world. Many thinkers have compared the Internet to this worldwide web, although this seems like a trivialization of what he meant. For Teilhard the intent was much deeper than shared information; his vision embraced an intensifying communion of compassion and understanding.

"ESCAPE THROUGH THE EXCESS OF CONSCIOUSNESS"[2]

Teilhard had his own unique way of looking at the journey of evolution that involves the whole human and non-human Universe. For him, the entire Cosmos is on its way, through the process of cosmic evolution, to becoming spirit or love. He believed that matter itself will be transformed into spirit through a process he called hominization. Through human consciousness, matter will rise into spirit. The human mind is the medium of transformation.

1. Teilhard de Chardin, *Future of Mankind*, chap. 3, sec. 2.
2. Ibid., chap. 22, para. 22.

One of the shocking things about Teilhard's thought is the central position he gives the human race within his scheme. He saw human beings as the apex of evolution, the ones through whom the entire Cosmos would find resolution. He has been roundly criticized for this anthropocentrism, but I have to admit I find a lot of sense in what he says if I make a few adjustments informed by the new cosmology. The way I see it, as far as we know, humans are the means of fulfillment so far in the evolution of the world. This is not to say they are particularly worthy or fitting vehicles for the world's ascent, but simply that they are the most complex, evolved life form on Earth, and we do not know of any life forms beyond the Earth. There may be sentient beings in the Universe far more advanced than we are, and the human race may well destroy itself along with its habitat on Earth—the specter of ecological disaster had not yet raised its head when Teilhard was writing. However, as far as we know now, human beings are the realm where consciousness and compassion seem to be growing. I feel sure that if we wipe ourselves off the face of the Earth, all that we have accomplished will not be lost but will be saved by the Universe, and when the next species of self-reflexive beings arise, they will be a quantum leap ahead of where we left off. Or perhaps the evolution of the Cosmos will be focused on an entirely different planet—indeed, perhaps it is already going on within many solar systems beyond the reach of our intelligence. So, it is not so much that humans are at the cutting edge of evolution, but self-reflexive consciousness is. It is the rise of consciousness that is important. Also, Swimme and Berry continually remind us that human beings do not exist in isolation but are a product of everything that has gone before them. We *are* the Cosmos, and anything we accomplish is a cosmic accomplishment. We are the Universe reflecting on itself and growing toward God. As I read Teilhard, I keep these things in mind. If he were alive today, perhaps he would have widened his locus of transformation to include these possibilities, but as things stand, I am content to see his hominization of the Universe in a panoramic, cosmic sense.

If we recall Swimme's shorthand for Teilhard's vision, that the direction of evolution is from matter to life to spirit to God, we can say that matter is being gradually transformed into spirit though the process of hominization, which means that evolution is now focused on the transformation of human consciousness.[3] All the elements and energies of the

---

3. Bridle, "Divinization of Cosmos."

world are taken up by humans and brought forward to a further dimension of evolution. God is drawing the Cosmos toward fulfillment through the rise of consciousness into spirit. Teilhard believed that eventually the Universe, through human consciousness, would reach such a heightened state of unity that it would pass from matter into spirit, and that transformation would constitute the fulfillment of time and existence. In Christian terms, this is the Parousia or the Second Coming. Teilhard speaks of it as a "spiritual escape through the excess of consciousness."[4]

BECOMING LOVE THROUGH CHRIST

Most importantly, it is love, which has always existed in the Universe, that needs to be hominized. Probably the most famous, most frequently quoted piece of Teilhard's writings refers to this human seizing of the power of love that has been gradually rising in the Universe within the movement toward greater complexity/consciousness. I have already quoted it, but it bears repeating once more: "Someday, after we have mastered the winds, the waves, the tides and gravity, we shall harness the energies of love. And then for the second time in the history of the world, man will have discovered fire."[5]

Teilhard's essential vision was that love is the driving force of evolution and what transforms matter into spirit. When human beings choose to act in a loving way, they move the world toward its goal; conversely, when they reject love they move the world backwards into matter. Free will, like consciousness, has become a property of the Universe through the evolution of human beings. He believed that God, the source of love, is both propelling us forward and drawing us to fulfillment from the future, which he called the Omega Point. By this he meant the time when the whole Cosmos will be one with love.

So far, only one side of the story has been told—that of the direction of evolving creation. When placed within the context of faith in the Creator, it takes on its true depth and meaning for Teilhard. All creation is destined to become a part of God and is already suffused with the divine for those who can truly see. Teilhard was not a panentheist thinker—he did not see the world as already part of God but as moving toward divinization. Yet, for him the very rocks cried out with the presence of God,

4. Teilhard de Chardin, *Future of Mankind*, chap. 3, sec. 2.
5. Teilhard de Chardin, "Evolution of Chastity," 86–87.

and he spoke mystically about the future fulfillment of the world as some-how already present. This fracturing of a sense of time is typical of mysti-cism. The Omega Point, which is the point of realization for creation, is also mysteriously present within time from its inception: "By the 'Omega Point,' Teilhard meant a Universe that had become God . . . He regarded the Omega Point as two things. It is an event that the Universe is moving toward in the future. But what he also imagined, which is difficult for us to really conceive, is that even though the Omega Point is in the future, it is also exerting a force on the present . . . In some mysterious way, the future is right here."[6]

The Omega Point is achieved through Christ, who is the alpha and omega of existence in Teilhard's vision of reality. Teilhard's worldview was centered on the universal Christ through whom all things were made and through whom everything reaches its completion.[7] The cosmic Christ, within Christian doctrine, is the locus of divine creation. In Trinitarian terms, the Father created the Universe through the Son. Traditional Christianity teaches that Christ redeemed the world through sacrificial love and will bring it to an end through the Parousia , the Second Coming of Christ at the end of time. Teilhard wove his evolutionary eschatol-ogy around these beliefs.[8] For Teilhard then, Christ is the power of love, which animates and drives the process of evolution until God becomes all in all.

It is love, which causes the movement of the Universe toward unity, toward God. Love is the "principle of unification" causing all things to converge.[9] This is not to say that humans have no choice in the matter. They have to learn to love one another and allow a single body of collec-tive humanity to emerge. Considering that Teilhard's vision was forged in the midst of two world wars, he could hardly be accused of ignoring the devastatingly destructive side of humanity. He stared into it—he was a stretcher-bearer in World War I—and yet he saw the rise of conscious-

6. Bridle, "The Divinization of Cosmos."

7. Col. 1:15–16 (NRSV).

8. I do not, personally, connect the Cosmic Christ with Jesus of Nazareth. The Cosmic Christ is a symbol of the creating, saving, transforming aspect of God. I do not find this title helpful and prefer to simply think of God creating the world and drawing it home to a full participation in divinity. When I read Teilhard, I have to imagine things more simply.

9. Teilhard de Chardin, *Future of Mankind*, chap. 3, sec. 4.

ness toward compassion and love that he believed to be the destiny of the human species. Today, our world still suffers the consequences of hatred, narrow vision, and selfishness, yet it is possible to distinguish within a macro perspective the slow but inexorable rise of compassion. As we have already seen, many modern thinkers believe that we are on the cusp of a rise in consciousness—or as Teilhard would say a reinvention of the human.

It is comforting to know that we are not alone in our struggle toward unity. Swimme says that the Universe is luring us toward wholeness, and Teilhard asserts that the cosmic Christ is empowering and drawing us on. No matter how we envision it, it is crucial to perceive that something much greater than our individual selves is leading us to transformation. In the end though, as always, we are free to chose life or death: "Even under the irresistible compulsion of the pressures causing it to unite, [hu]mankind will only find and shape itself if [humans] can learn to love one another in the very act of drawing closer."[10] For Teilhard, as for traditional Christian theology, there is no loss of personhood when the individual enters the realm of fulfillment. Personhood is not subsumed into the being of God. Teilhard scholar Bernice Bruteau explains that "our personal energies do not merge or become submerged in some amorphous whole. We do not acquire a kind of oceanic sense of being swallowed up in a great All. Quite the contrary: subjectively, it feels rather like an intensification of individuality."[11]

The debate over whether entities maintain or lose their identity after death remains contentious and provocative, ranging through all the world's religions and philosophies. From his standpoint, straddling the worlds of science and spirituality, Brian Swimme proposes that when we die we become part of the Cosmos in a new way that retains the essence of our individuality: "What is retained (in death) is the beauty of a particular life . . . We become part of a huge community . . . this is the traditional doctrine of the communion of the saints . . . I think the resurrected body is coextensive with the Cosmos; it isn't a loss of identity; it's actually like a new hue or a new tone."[12] As Teilhard asserts, in the afterlife "each drop [of the ocean of eternity] will still be conscious of being itself."[13] I find

10. Ibid., chap. 15, sec. 1.

11. Edelstein and Daly, "A Song."

12. U.S. Catholics Eds., "Where does your faith."

13. Teilhard de Chardin, *Future of Mankind*, conclusion, sec. 1.

this thrilling—to imagine an eternity of transformed consciousness. Somehow, the little speck that is me contributes to the vast whole.

THE END OF THE WORLD

Teilhard tried to imagine what the Parousia would be like. His vision arose from dream and intuition rather than any quasi-scientific factuality. He did not intend his ideas to be read in any other way. The end of the world is beyond human understanding:

> It is difficult to imagine what form the ending of a World might take. A sidereal disaster would correspond nearly enough to our individual deaths. But this would entail the ending of the Earth rather than of the Cosmos, and it is the Cosmos itself that must disappear. The more I ponder this mystery the more it assumes in my dreams the aspect of a 'turning inward' of consciousness, an eruption of interior life, an ecstasy. There is no need for us to rack our brains in trying to understand how the immensity of the material Universe might vanish. It is enough that the spirit should be reversed, that it should enter another sphere, for the face of the World to be instantly altered.[14]

In Teilhard's vision, creation will be brought to the "paroxysm of its aptitude for union," and that will somehow tip it over into a new state of being.[15] This will be the Parousia. It will be a moment of "terrifying spiritual pressure" where humans will have to make the definitive choice of stepping back into pluralism due to the urgings of the ego, or moving forward into communion—losing themselves only to find themselves in the abyss of God.[16] Ultimately though, the end of the world will be an experience of tremendous, undreamt of joy and peace, as the Cosmos finds its home in the heart of love: "Like a vast tide, the Being will have dominated the trembling of all beings. The extraordinary adventure of the World will have ended in the bosom of a tranquil ocean, of which, however, each drop will still be conscious of being itself. The dream of every mystic will have found its full and proper fulfillment."[17]

---

14. Ibid., conclusion, sec. 1.

15. Ibid., conclusion, sec. 1.

16. Ibid., conclusion, sec. 1.

17. Ibid., conclusion, sec. 1.

18

Eternal Journey into Deeper Love

I T SEEMS FITTING TO conclude this section by turning to metaphor and story once more as an entranceway into the mystery of the far future. All theology is, in the end, metaphorical, especially so theology that considers life after death. It bears repeating that the imagination may be the best tool humans have to approach ultimate meaning. C.S. Lewis wrote some wonderful stories about the transformation of the temporal world into the eternal, and we will look at his books *The Great Divorce* and *The Last Battle* (which ends *The Chronicles of Narnia* series) to give our imaginations a chance to stretch.

A DREAM OF HEAVEN AND HELL

The Great Divorce is a tale about a dream about heaven and hell. The dream begins in a gray town, which is dingy, dark, and rainy and inhabited by quarrelsome, unhappy people. The main protagonist of the story, the dreamer, is standing in a line of these people waiting for a bus. After a period of time that is so fraught with disagreement and violence that most of the queue does not board it, the bus arrives and takes them up out of the gray town into a land of almost unbearable brilliance, where the travelers become as insubstantial as ghosts. This land, which is full of light and beauty, causes pain to the ghosts because everything in it is too real for them. The very grass causes them suffering because it hurts their shadowy feet with its concreteness. Out of this gorgeous country come magnificent, radiant people who know the ghosts and try to welcome them into their new home, but one by one, the unhappy phantoms find reasons why they cannot stay, and they choose to go back to the gray town on the bus. Their reasons are all to do with not being able to let go of ego, past hurt, delusion, or spite. It becomes apparent that they can only stay in the country of ultimate reality if they let go of all remnants of non-real-ity and become their true selves. Most of the ghosts are unwilling to do so, despite the encouragement of their beautiful friends.

The reader begins to realize that Lewis is writing about heaven and hell. Within the realm of "imaginative supposal" he communicates his vision of the human journey to the fullness of joy and the choices that decide their destiny.[1] In the story, the gray land is a symbol of purga-tory/hell, and in it reside people who have died and have not yet had the courage to overcome their faults or the will to choose heaven. All the inhabitants have the opportunity to live in heaven, provided by the daily bus, but many cannot let go of the barriers and burdens that keep them from becoming real, and the gray land becomes hell, finally, for those who have given up all notion of getting on the bus. Hell is the antithesis of reality. The dreamer is shown hell from the perspective of heaven by his guide, who points to a tiny crack in the ground of the beautiful country and explains that this is how the bus came into heaven. He explains: "All Hell is smaller than one pebble of your Earthly world: but it is smaller than one atom of *this* world, the Real World."[2]

It is the imaginative description of heaven in *The Great Divorce* that is most important in the context of this chapter. We realize that "[h]eaven is reality itself."[3] It is the pinnacle of life lived within the fullness of love, and yet this completeness continues, paradoxically, to become fuller, rich-er and deeper. It seems that the word *full* is a human construct, limited by the experience that is available within this finite realm. We can only dream what full might mean in an infinite world. Polkinghorne comes to mind in his contention that perfection is a much more dynamic process than its Greek heritage allows, and that the heavenly realm is not static but an ever richer reality.

The dreamer realizes that the heavenly guides have made a real sac-rifice to come back to the edge of heaven in order to try to persuade the ghosts to stay, for heaven becomes more and more glorious as it is entered into. It is ongoing, and yet Lewis makes the point very strongly that there is a complete separation between heaven and hell, a divorce rather than the marriage of heaven and hell Blake wrote about, which is the work Lewis

1. Lewis, *Great Divorce*, 9.

2. Ibid., 113.

3. Ibid., 63.

took his inspiration from. When a ghost chooses heaven, a transformation takes place that is akin to a new creation. A core identity is maintained, but the past dynamics of previous existence pass away. Neither Earthly existence nor hellish existence can simply become heaven. It is a new creation. C. S. Lewis answers the argument from O'Murchu and process thinkers that the ongoing nature of heaven might mean a continuation of the dynamics we currently know about in the Universe: the dynamics of paradox, tension, and opposites, the supposition that suffering may continue in heaven in order that novelty and growth may continue. For Lewis it is necessary to let go of pain and suffering to enter heaven. Here Lewis echoes the promise that runs throughout scripture and is revealed consummately in Jesus' resurrection, that every tear will be wiped away, that all creation will be made new: "See. . . . he will wipe every tear from their eyes. Death will be no more; mourning and crying and pain will be no more, for the first things have passed away."[4]

If suffering and pain are to be considered as integral to life after death, then one could say with Lewis that 'hell has vetoed heaven.' This is made clear in one of the stories within the dream, which is about a woman called Sarah Smith who is referred to in heaven as the Lady because of her overwhelming goodness and beauty. The Lady is approached by a phantom called Frank who had been her husband on Earth. Their marriage had not been a satisfying one because Frank had given very little to it, being bound up inside his own neediness and self-concern. Frank, as he had done many times on Earth, tries to get the Lady to stroke his ego by saying that she misses and needs him. The Lady tells Frank that the love she experiences now is not needy and egotistical, that indeed she is a part of the reality of love: "I am in Love, and out of it I will not go."[5] She does her best to encourage Frank to let go of his shadow of love and enter the real thing, but he insists on returning to hell. He wants her to go to hell with him out of pity, but she insists that she cannot and will not go. The dreamer, watching all this, wonders aloud to his guide if she should have gone with Frank, and if the joy of heaven is incomplete if someone, somewhere, is still suffering. He is told that "hell cannot veto heaven," that heaven is the fullness of joy and cannot be tinged by sadness.[6] If suffering

---

4. Rev. 214 (NRSV).

5. Lewis, *Great Divorce*, 109.

6. Ibid., 111.

is to be considered as still a part of heaven, then does heaven not lose its defining nature? If this is the case, is heaven not vetoed by hell? An ongoing realm, where suffering is the price of novelty and growth, negates the reality of heaven, which is the realm of ever-deepening joy and love and beauty.

At the end of the dream in *The Great Divorce* a moment comes when the dawn, which has been gradually arriving in the beautiful land, shoots its first rays from beyond the far mountains and this signals the end of time and the end of choices or movement from hell to heaven. Purgatory and hell are no more as joy becomes all in all: "The Eastern side of every tree-trunk grew bright. Shadows deepened. All the time there had been bird noises, trillings, chatterings, and the like; but now suddenly the full chorus was poured from every branch; cocks were crowing, there was music of hounds, and horns; above all this ten thousand tongues of men and woodland angels and the wood itself sang. 'It comes! It comes!' they sang. 'Sleepers awake! It comes, it comes, it comes.'"[7] At the end of time in this Universe there will be no more evolution as we know it now because all things will have become God.

THE REALLY REAL

In his book *The Last Battle*, Lewis writes in a similar vein about the ongoing nature of heaven. He concludes the adventures of the mythical land of Narnia by describing the transformation of the land into a new creation within the home of Aslan, the lion who is the marvelous God figure of the Narnia series. The impact of the last part of this last book in the series can only be really felt if the reader has been caught up in the struggles and adventures of the characters of Narnia. One feels a tremendous denouement occurring as Lewis brings all of this to glorious resolution. As the land and all the heroes of Narnia are transformed from the shadow of themselves into the really real, it becomes apparent that there is no possibility of ever experiencing fear, limitation, or sadness ever again, no end to the deepening of delight that is experienced: "But for them it was only the beginning of the real story. All their life in this world and all their adventures in Narnia had only been the cover and the title page: now at last they were beginning Chapter One of the Great Story which no one

7. Ibid., 194.

on Earth has read: which goes on forever: in which every chapter is better than the one before."[8]

It is hard to put into words how Lewis's stories of hope and promise make me feel. I urge the reader to go to the originals to receive the full impact of their beauty and mystery. Perhaps I could sum up their effect on me by saying that they give me an overwhelming sense that life has a wonderful and consummate destiny, that all the history of the Cosmos, all past moments of anguish and delight will find their answer, their reason within the heart of God.

THE GOD WHO PROMISES

What does God promise? God promises a worthy destination to the pilgrim Universe, which is journeying toward wholeness. God promises to be present with creation on every step of this journey, to suffer with it, to guide it and lure it home, to provide ultimate justice for created beings who suffer injustice, to embrace and save every effort made to live in love, and to give the fullness of reality to all those who have struggled to become real. God promises that the Universe will become one in love with the one who is love.

Who, therefore, is the God of promise? God is the power that can give ultimate fulfillment. God is the faithful, patient, long-suffering fellow traveler who experiences the pain of an incomplete world, but God is also the destination, the homecoming of creation. God is the wisdom and beauty that can guide and attract all beings into the heart of life. God is justice, remembering and redeeming every cry of pain, giving the fullness of life to all those who have struggled to love, while regretfully allowing the unjust and unworthy to follow their own path and fade into non-existence. God is reality itself, sharing radiant life with all who choose to become real. God is the lover who invites all creation into the ever-growing ecstasy of consummation, into the always-surprising extravagance of the great feast.

One thing that God is not is impersonal. It would be quite easy to lose sight of the personal aspect of divinity in trying to distance ourselves from the notion of God being a person, like a human, only better, up in the sky somewhere. I do not believe that God is a person who has human emotions and gets angry, yet I think it is vital to preserve the re-

8. Lewis, *Last Battle*, 172.

lational and personal aspect of divinity. I cannot become intimate with a something—a force or energy—even if I conceive of that something as the source and life force of the Universe. For me, one of the treasures of Christianity is the personal nature of God, made explicit in Jesus.

Paul Tillich wrote extensively on the idea of the personal in God. In *Theology of Culture*, he answers the argument that a personal God is incompatible with scientific knowledge by positing the idea that it is a symbol of the mysterious or numinous character of the Cosmos that both science and religion point to. He argues that science is quite right to reject the notion of a supernatural being who arbitrarily sets aside the laws of nature and is an object or being alongside other beings. The word *person* can only be seen in a symbolic sense to refer to the personal dimension of reality. Tillich argues that in humans the Universe has reached its highest expression of being so far; that through self-reflexive consciousness the capacity for relationships of tremendous depth has emerged that can only be expressed in the idea of the personal. If humans are capable of relationships that allow mutual in-depth communication of persons, then how can God be less than personal? For Tillich, God is "supra-personal:"[9]

> The depth of being cannot be symbolized by objects taken from a realm which is lower than the personal, from the realm of things or sub-personal living beings. The supra-personal is not an "It," or more exactly, it is a "He" as much as it is an "It," and it is above both of them. But if the "He" element is left out, the "It" element transforms the alleged supra-personal into a sub-personal, as usually happens in monism and pantheism. And such a neutral sub-personal cannot grasp the center of our personality; it can satisfy our aesthetic feeling or our intellectual needs, but it cannot convert our will, it cannot overcome our loneliness, anxiety, and despair. For as the philosopher Shelling says: "Only a person can heal a person." This is the reason that the symbol of the Personal God is indispensable for living religion.[10]

A personal God evokes trust, which is the most essential response that creation can make, trust that God can and will fulfill all the promises that are felt at the heart of life. Theology can only dream about the nature of the ultimate destiny of the Universe. Trust bids creation to believe that God will save and transform all who want to be saved and are worthy of

9. Tillich, *Theology of Culture*, 131.

10. Ibid., 131–32.

being saved. Trust bids us believe in the promise that is written deepest down in the human heart—that love will be all in all; God will be all in all. I do not think it is sentimental to suggest that the human heart does not lie. I believe that the deep, inchoate longing that human beings experience is not just the product of wishful thinking or an inability to accept the harshness of existential truth, but an expression, or an incarnation, of the erotic longing and pervasive restlessness of the Universe itself. It points towards the future, feeling its way along, groping just as evolution does—following its allurements, as Swimme would say. The happy ending that we always want on the end of every story is not because we are unrealistic dreamers, but because we know the truth deep down. Some people, whom we call martyrs, are so sure of this that they are willing to give up their lives for it. Along with them, generations of simple, ordinary people make sense of their lives and live lovingly and courageously within the enfolding embrace of this promise. Their trust must be answered by the realization of their hopes and dreams.

Despite the often-painful paradox of existence within the present realm, we can join with the medieval mystic Julian of Norwich, who lived during the terrible time of the Great Plague, in trusting God's power to save. Despite all evidence to the contrary, she was able to hear God saying to creation: "I may make all things well, and I can make all things well, and I shall make all things well, and I will make all things well; and you will see yourself that every kind of thing will be well."[11]

11. Julian of Norwich, *Showings*, 229.

Bibliography

Augros, Robert M., and George N. Stanciu. *The New Story of Science*. New York: Bantam, 1984.

Augustine. *Confessions*. Translated by Rex Warner. New York: Penguin, 1963.

Barbour, Ian G. *Religion in an Age of Science*. San Francisco: Harper, 1990. No pages. Online: http://www.religion-online.org/showbook.asp?title=2237.

Berry, Thomas. *The Dream of the Earth*. San Francisco: Sierra Club, 1988.

———. *The Great Work: Our Way Into the Future*. New York: Bell Tower, 1999.

———. "The Spirituality of the Earth." In *Liberating Life: Contemporary Approaches in Ecological Theology*, edited by C. Birch et al., 1990. No pages. Online: http://www.religion-online.org/showarticle.asp?title=2313.

Berry, Thomas, and Brian Swimme. *The Universe Story*. New York: HarperCollins, 1992.

Boorman, Charley, and Ewan McGregor. *Long Way Round*. DVD. Elixir Productions/ Image Wizard Media, 2004.

Borg, Marcus, J. *Meeting Jesus for the First Time*. New York: HarperCollins, 1994.

Bridle, Susan. "The Divinization of the Cosmos: An Interview with Brian Swimme on Pierre Teilhard de Chardin." *What Is Enlightenment? Magazine*, 19. (2001). No pages. Online: http://www.wie.org/j19/teilhard.asp?pf=1.

Bush, George W. "Address to the Nation on the Terrorist Attacks." *Public Papers of the Presidents* 2 (September 11, 2001): 1099–1100. Online:http://www.presidency.ucsb. edu/ws/index.php?pid=58057&st=Address+to+the+Nation+on+the+Terrorist+Att acks&st1=.

Campbell, Joseph. *The Power of Myth*. With Bill Moyers. Edited by Betty Sue Flowers. New York: Doubleday, 1988.

Capra, Fritjof. *The Tao of Physics*. 4th edition. Boston: Shambhala, 2000.

Cerami, Vincenzo and Roberto Benigni. *Life is Beautiful*. Movie. Directed by Roberto Benigni. New York: Miramax, 2007.

Dawkins, Richard. *River Out Of Eden*. New York: Basic Books, 1995.

———. *The Selfish Gene*. New York: Oxford University Press, 1976.

Dillard, Annie. *For the Time Being*. New York: Knopf, 1999.

Edelstein, Amy, and Ellen Daly. "A Song That Goes on Singing: An Interview with Dr. Beatrice Bruteau." *What Is Enlightenment? Magazine*, 21. (2002). No pages. Online: http://www.wie.org/j21/bruteau.asp?page=2.

Ferris, Timothy. *The Whole Shebang*. New York: Touchstone, 1997.

Gibran, Kahlil. *The Prophet*. New York: Alfred A Knopf, 1984. First published 1923.

Haught, John F. *The Cosmic Adventure: Science, Religion and the Quest for Purpose*. New York: Paulist Press, 1984. No pages. Online: http://www.religion-online.org/ showbook.asp?title=1948.

―――. *Mystery and Promise: A Theology of Revelation*. Collegeville, Minnesota: Liturgical Press, 1993. No pages. Online: http://www.religion-online.org/showbook. asp?title=1947.

Henderson, Charles P. *God and Science*. Louisville, Kentucky: John Knox, 1986. No pages. Online: http://www.godweb.org/chardin.htm.

Huther, Gerald. *The Compassionate Brain: How Empathy Creates Intelligence*. Boston: Trumpeter, 2006.

Jeffares A. Norman, editor. *W. B. Yeats Selected Poetry*. London: Macmillan, 1962.

Julian of Norwich. *Showings*. Translated by E. Colledge and J. Walsh, New York: Paulist Press, 1978.

Kennedy, John F. *Inaugral Address*. (January 20, 1961). Online: www.jfklibrary.org.

King, Thomas M. *Teilhard's Mysticism of Knowing*. New York: Seabury, 1981.

Knudtson, Peter and David Suzuki. *Wisdom of the Elders*. Toronto, Canada: Stoddart, 1992.

Lewis, Clive Staples. *The Great Divorce*. Glasgow: Collins, 1979. First published 1946 by Geoffrey Bles.

―――. *The Last Battle*. Glasgow: Collins, 1986. First published 1956 by The Bodley Head.

Lovelock, James. *The Ages of Gaia*. New York: Bantam/W. W. Norton, 1988.

Margulis, Lynne. *Symbiotic Planet: A New Look at Evolution*. Amherst, Massachusetts: Basic Books, 1998.

Mistry, Rohinton. *A Fine Balance*. Toronto, Canada: McClelland and Stewart, 1995.

Moltmann, Jürgen. *The Crucified God: The Cross of Jesus as the Foundation and Criticism of Christian Theology*. Translated by J. Bowden. New York: Harper and Row, 1974.

―――. *God in Creation: An Ecological Doctrine of Creation*. Translated by M. Kohl. London: SCM, 1985.

Nouwen, Henri. *With Open Hands*. Notre Dame, Indiana: Ave Maria, 1995.

O'Donahue, John. *Anam Cara*. New York: Cliff St, 1997.

―――. *Beauty: The Invisible Embrace*. New York: Perennial, 2004.

O'Murchu, Diarmuid. *Quantum Theology*. New York: Crossroad, 1997.

Pittenger, Norman. *The 'Last Things' in a Process Perspective*. London: Epworth, 1970. No pages. Online: http://www.religion-online.org/showbook.asp?title=2214.

Polkinghorne, John. "Eschatology: Some Questions and Some Insights from Science." In *The End of the World and the Ends of God: Science and Theology on Eschatology*, edited by John Polkinghorne and Michael Welker. Harrisburg, Pennsylvania: Trinity, 2000.

―――. *The God of Hope and the End of the World*. London: SPCK, 2002.

Polkinghorne, John, editor. *The Work of Love: Creation as Kenosis*. Cambridge: William B. Eerdman, 2001.

Polkinghorne, John, and Michael Welker, eds. *The End of the World and the Ends of God: Science and Theology on Eschatology*. Harrisburg, Pennsylvania: Trinity, 2000.

Rolston III, Holmes. *Genes, Genesis and God*. Cambridge, UK: Cambridge University Press, 1999.

―――. "Kenosis and Nature." In *The Work of Love: Creation as Kenosis*, Edited by John Polkinghorne. Cambridge: William B. Eerdman, 2001.

Sheldrake, Rupert. "Prayer: A Challenge for Science." *Noetic Sciences Review*, 30 (1994). No pages. Online: http://www.sheldrake.org/papers/Morphic/prayer_paper.html.

Southwell, Robert. "New Heaven, New War." No pages. Online: www.luminarium.org/renlit/newheaven.htm.

Suzuki, David. *The Sacred Balance*. Vancouver, British Columbia: Greystone, 1997.

Swimme, Brian. *Canticle to the Cosmos*. Audiocassette series. Boulder, Colorado: Sounds True Audio, 1990.

————. *The Hidden Heart of the Cosmos*. New York: Orbis, 1996.

————. *The Universe is a Green Dragon*. Santa Fe: Bear & Company, 1984.

Teilhard de Chardin, Pierre. "The Evolution of Chastity." In *Toward the Future*. London: Collins, 1975.

————. *The Future of Mankind*. New York and Evanston: Harper & Row, 1959. No pages. Online: http://www.religion-online.org/showbook.asp?title=2287.

————. *The Phenomenon of Man*. Translated by B. Wall. London: Collins, 1959. First published 1955 by Editions du Seuil.

Tillich, Paul. *Theology of Culture*. New York: Oxford University Press, 1959.

Tolle, Eckhart. *The Power of Now*. Vancouver, British Columbia: Namaste, 1997.

U.S. Catholic Eds. "Where does your faith fit in the cosmos?" Interview with Brian Swimme. *U.S. Catholic*. (June 1997). No pages. Online: http://www.thefreelibrary.com/Where+does+your+faith+fit+in+the+cosmos%3F-a019489108.

Ward, Keith. "Cosmos and Kenosis." In *The Work of Love: Creation as Kenosis,* edited by John Polkinghorne. Cambridge: William B. Eerdman, 2001.

Whitehead, Alfred North. *Adventures of Ideas*. New York: Free Press, 1967.

Wilber, Ken. *A Brief History of Everything*. Boston: Shambhala, 1996.

Zukav, Gary. *The Dancing Wu Li Masters*. New York: Morrow Quill, 1979.